Citizenship through Secondary Religious Educat

Religion has achieved an ever greater prominence in debates about citizenship at every level of cultural, economic, social and political life. *Citizenship through Secondary Religious Education* highlights some of the key issues surrounding citizenship for the teacher of religious education.

Some chapters focus on issues of historical as well as immediate relevance to teaching citizenship through religious education, and other chapters cover general critical and planning issues. Topics include:

- The open society and its enemies
- The politics of hell on earth
- Planning for citizenship
- Genocide
- Slavery
- Asylum
- Freedom of expression
- Freedom of religion and belief
- Sustainable development
- Women's rights
- The rights of indigenous peoples

Accessible and practical in style, this book will be invaluable to newly qualified and experienced teachers, as well as trainees. Those teaching citizenship and/or religious education as a second subject will also find the book an indispensable resource.

Liam Gearon is Reader in Education and Director of the Centre for Research in Human Rights at the University of Surrey Roehampton. He is also editor of *Learning to Teach Citizenship in the Secondary School*, published by RoutledgeFalmer in 2003.

Citizenship Education in Secondary Schools Series

Series Editor: John Moss

Canterbury Christ Church University College

Citizenship through Secondary Geography
Edited by David Lambert and Paul Machon

Citizenship through Secondary History
James Arthur, Ian Davies, Andrew Wrenn, Terry Haydn and David Kerr

Citizenship through Secondary English
John Moss

Citizenship through Secondary Religious Education

Liam Gearon

RoutledgeFalmer
Taylor & Francis Group

LONDON AND NEW YORK

First published 2004
by RoutledgeFalmer
11 New Fetter Lane, London EC4P 4EE

Simultaneously published in the USA and Canada
by RoutledgeFalmer
29 West 35th Street, New York, NY 10001

RoutledgeFalmer is an imprint of the Taylor & Francis Group

© 2004 Liam Gearon

Typeset in Baskerville by Keystroke, Jacaranda Lodge, Wolverhampton
Printed and bound in Great Britain by St Edmundsbury Press,
Bury St Edmunds, Suffolk

British Library Cataloguing in Publication Data
A catalogue record for this book is available from the British Library

Library of Congress Cataloging in Publication Data
A catalog record for this book has been requested

ISBN 0–415–29812–1

Contents

Boxes

Acknowledgements

Texts and extracts taken from UN websites (including UNHCHR and UNHCR) are reprinted by permission of the United Nations, publisher of the authentic text. The QCA citizenship unit on conflict (pp. 15–21) is reprinted by permission of QCA. For all such sources, the reader is strongly encouraged to refer to the full text of official documents and related sources as suggested throughout this book. Any unintended failures of acknowledgement will be rectified in future editions.

The City of God

Citizenship through religious education

News stories concerning the occupation and subsequent siege of the Church of the Nativity in Bethlehem, around the time of Easter 2001, presented some of the most compelling reasons why religious education needs to make a constructive contribution to citizenship. Whatever judgements we make of the situation, of all instances of Israeli incursions into the Palestinian Authority Territory, those into Bethlehem seemed to provide the sharpest focus for the conflict between worldviews – political, religious, social, cultural, economic. The clash of worldviews *in extremis*? Six months later we had the headlines detailing events from the bombing of the twin towers of the World Trade Center in New York on 11 September 2001.

Is religion incidental or central to this violence? Is religion, to use a cliché, part of the problem or part of the solution? However we answer such questions, religion is part of the discussion about citizenship at every level. What religious education can add to discussions of citizenship is to set the historical and contemporary struggles of politics into a wider ethical, existential, even theological context.

Yet if religions provide the oldest of humankind's systems of moral and philosophical order, a post-Enlightenment world does not always regard religion as a progressive influence upon either individuals or societies. How untainted have religious histories been in terms of repression and persecution, especially in the history of western imperialism, and particularly in relation to indigenous peoples – from the Americas through to Australasia? To what extent has religious intolerance generated genocide and justified the use of torture? Have religions ever ennobled slavery? What has been the religious record in terms of freedom of expression? What are the present attitudes of religions in relation to minorities? Do religions give equal status to men and women? If a political party had the blemished record of some religious traditions, would it find free and democratic political support today?

It might of course be easy to take the secularist agenda and suggest that religion has to make all the running in the citizenship stakes. This would be an error. Religions have created amongst the greatest art and architecture, written and inspired the greatest literature, produced the most profound existential, philosophical and theological thinking, and, perhaps amongst all things, formulated ethical and moral systems which have transformed the state of human beings, allowing the order of the modern world.

It was Saint Augustine who wrote the magisterial *City of God* concerning a vision of political order governed by theological principles. It was a Christian martyr, Saint Thomas More, who wrote *Utopia* before his execution by an English king. Religious educators need to re-examine some of these political traditions within the context of citizenship. Despite expectations of a decline in the influence of religion in the world of politics and public life, religion in the twenty-first century (for better or worse) has maintained its place in global governance.

Of course, our opening remarks relating events of 2001 – from Bethlehem to New York – might convince some readers that a secular vision is preferable to the interference of religion. Yet we cannot ignore the continuing influence of what some have pejoratively called the 'clash of civilizations' (Huntington 1993).

Let's take and test another year, 2002. What, for instance, of this pivotal year when National Curriculum citizenship was introduced in England? We had the continuing war on terror, with all its contested religious and cultural undertones; the ongoing rise of the far right with its intolerance of religious and cultural minorities; we had the Bali bombing to remind us that what is at stake is costing lives. And there are ongoing situations of social and especially economic injustice, particularly the growing divide between rich and poor, which lead millions to live lives of absolute depriva- tion, which remains an unmet challenge to religious believers who have faith in a just and good God – the age-old problem of evil, the suffering of the innocent and the challenge of theodicy.

The human struggle for 'cities of God' on earth has led to centuries of political and theological disillusionment: theocracies like any utopias are illusive, and the path to their attainment fraught with danger. Wars of religion have caused arguably more bloodshed than any other form of struggle, manifest as they often are in disguised terms of ethnicity, culture, ideology. The task of the religious educator is to grasp and confront such issues with the expertise that only they possess within the school community. From numerically small indigenous and tribal traditions to traditions with immense numbers of adherents (Christianity and Islam both exceed a billion), religious educators have an understanding and appreciation of the great contribution religions have made to human civilisations over millennia and continue to make today. Religious educators also have the knowledge and skills to inform citizenship–religious debate through insights into religious history, into conflicts between religious and ideological systems, and knowledge of theology, philosophy and ethics.

Given the relationship between religion and citizenship, politics in the broadest sense, religious educators have little choice but to take a professional interest in citizenship. This book is designed to provide some starting points for the teacher of religious education interested in developing expertise in the field.

How the book works

Citizenship through Secondary Religious Education provides a theoretical context and a range of practical applications for the teacher of citizenship as well as religious education specialists to explore themes of local, national and international, political significance.

The book is divided into two major sections. Chapters 1 and 2 of Part I address generic issues about the involvement of religion with the world of politics, as well as the political dimensions of religious education. Using the QCA Model Syllabuses for Religious Education and the National Curriculum Order as reference points, Chapter 1 highlights a number of potential areas for collaboration between the two subjects. Chapter 2 develops an approach to citizenship through religious education by means of human rights in national and international contexts, focusing on both rights and responsibilities. Chapter 3 of Part I develops practical strategies in planning to teach religious education through citizenship, within and beyond the classroom. Each chapter has a 'Question, discuss, research' section to facilitate further, critical reflection and investigation.

Part II of the book, covering Chapters 4 to 11, provides more in-depth treatment of 'rights, wrongs and responsibilities' and issues of historical and pressing, contemporary significance: genocide (Chapter 4); asylum (Chapter 5); slavery (Chapter 6); freedom of expression (Chapter 7); freedom of religion and belief (Chapter 8); economic rights, environmental responsibilities and sustainable development (Chapter 9); women's rights (Chapter 10); and the rights of indigenous peoples (Chapter 11). In addition to a 'Question, discuss, research' section, each of the chapters in Part II provides outline 'Planning notes' linking National Curriculum citizenship to key themes in religious education as well as theme-related attainment targets, skills and processes, and attitudes.

Part I

Citizenship and religious education: critical contexts and planning issues

Chapter 1

The Open Society and Its Enemies

Citizenship and religious education

Introduction

Events like 11 September 2001 in the United States and the Bali bombing in November 2002 tell us that the world is not always unified by a common vision of how to order society. Since the beginning of the new millennium terror in the name of religion – with claims and counter-claims that such terror is not part of the tradition – has shown that far from disappearing from the public domain into a post-Enlightenment, privatised domain, religion is still 'out there'. In our discussions of religious education and citizenship there is something fundamental at stake about how modern societies should operate.

This chapter is an attempt to present in simple form the basic parameters of potential conflict and co-operation *vis-à-vis* religious education and citizenship, taking as fundamental the premise that these parameters will reflect current and historical political realities. It is in real political histories – in the UK, Europe and globally – that religion impacts upon notions of citizenship. We might usefully begin our study with a review of generic issues in citizenship education and research. From this basis we can then proceed to an examination of citizenship in relation to religious education. The premise for this chapter – and indeed this book – is that citizenship's respect for democratic freedoms is a form of protection for the ideals of tolerance and understanding so fundamental to religious education – a notion freely borrowed from Karl Popper, elaborated in *The Open Society and Its Enemies*.

Crick and National Curriculum citizenship

Citizenship has strong roots in personal, social and health education (PSE/PSHE), with which it is still formally associated (Best *et al.* 1995; Best 1999, 2002). Citizenship remains a part of the framework for PSHE in primary and secondary schools, with non-statutory guidance for key stages 1–2 and statutory effect in key stages 3–4 (DfEE 1999; QCA 2000a; Best 2002). Guidance on its implementation in secondary schools is well supported by QCA (2000b, 2001c, 2001d, 2001e, 2001f, 2001g, 2001h).

What we can call implicit citizenship also has antecedents from the 1970s onwards in relatively marginal initiatives in peace education, global studies, human rights education, and political education. With the advent of National Curriculum citizenship many of the areas previously classified under such titles shifted towards formal and explicit identification with citizenship. The most prominent review of related research at this transitional phase linked citizenship to values education (Taylor 1999; Halstead and Taylor 2001) The review of values-based research by Halstead and Taylor (2000) focused on five areas, with related research questions upon which their summary of available evidence was then based:

- Social background research
- The development of values through the life of the school

> How significant is the development of early moral emotions?
> What does 'caring' mean and how does it contribute to children's moral development?
> How far do school councils help young people to understand their rights and responsibilities as citizens?
> Does the involvement of pupils in the formation of classroom rules and social policies on discipline help them develop the motivation to behave responsibly?
> What kinds of influence can extra-curricular activities have on the behaviour and attitudes of children and young people?
> How far does the example set by teachers intentionally or otherwise influence the developing values and attitudes of their pupils?
> What does spiritual development mean?
> How can schools foster the values of non-discrimination and equal opportunities?

- Theoretical framework and strategies

> How can schools contribute to the character development of students?
> What specific strategies and programmes for the development of moral reasoning have been effective in school?
> How do personal narratives help teachers to understand and influence the moral development of young people?
> What contribution can the subjects of the National Curriculum make to the development of pupils' values and attitudes?
> What can religious education and personal and social education contribute to pupils' developing attitudes and values?
> How do the cross-curricular themes contribute to the development of pupils' values, attitudes and personal qualities?
> How effective is circle time in helping pupils to develop self-esteem and to clarify their own attitudes and values?
> What other teaching and learning methods have been found effective in influencing pupils' attitudes and behaviour?

- Curriculum and teaching methods

> What methods have proved effective in identifying developments in pupils' values and attitudes?

How can school effectiveness be evaluated in terms of the development of pupils' values and attitudes?

• Assessing and evaluating the development of pupils' values.

The sets of conclusions, in the form of research implications for teachers, for school policy, for inspection and for future research, are reproduced in Box 1.1.

Box 1.1
Citizenship-related research

Research implications for teachers
The research suggests that teachers should:

• build, where appropriate, on the foundations of moral development laid in the home and continue to seek partnerships with parents and other carers;
• pay due attention to the development of moral reasoning while not neglecting children's emotional and spiritual development;
• encourage children's active involvement in the running of the school community;
• aim for consistency in reinforcing the school's fundamental values;
• reflect on their own values and on the appropriateness of the example they set through their personal and professional conduct;
• encourage children to take part in a variety of activities which develop character and personal qualities, and provide opportunities for them to reflect on the moral issues which arise in these activities;
• ensure that the learning that occurs through their relationships with their pupils through peer interactions and through the life of the school is as positive as possible;
• reflect on the potential within school subjects and cross-curricular themes to raise questions of value;
• explore different methods for developing pupils' values, attitudes, and personal qualities;
• help pupils to develop a sense of their own moral identity and to become gradually more aware of the complex and controversial nature of many moral values;
• focus on specific aims in values education, directed at specific learning outcomes;
• develop methods of measuring and recording pupils' growth and development in these areas.

Research implications for school policy and practice
The research demonstrates the importance of:

• responding sensitively to the diverse and possibly irreconcilable expectations of national education policy, local communities, parents and pupils themselves, in the light of teachers' personal views and professional expertise;

continued

- working towards shared values, which are given a high profile and made explicit in a range of school policies, structures and procedures understood and owned by all members of the school community;
- developing a whole-school approach to values education, drawing on clear and coherent theoretical frameworks and strategies;
- engaging in ongoing reflection on and review of school life, the curriculum, teaching methods and partnerships with parents and communities to raise awareness of values issues.

Research implications for school inspection

In examining school provision and practices in the development of values, attitudes and personal qualities within the national framework for inspection, inspectors need to consider evaluation criteria and what counts as evidence for their judgements in the light of . . . research evidence.

Directions for future research

Although we have amassed a very large amount of both conceptual and empirical research evidence in this review, it has become clear that the researchers' agenda is not always the same as the practitioners' agenda. Some areas of school practice are notably under-researched, and these include areas inspectors are currently required to pay special attention in evaluating pupils' spiritual, moral, social and cultural development. In particular, there is little research evidence about how collective worship and teacher example influence pupils' development. There is much more research on moral and social development than on the relatively new domains of spiritual and cultural development, which are still undergoing conceptual clarification. There is also a shortage of experimental research and evaluations of programmes in the UK. The quality of available research is mixed, and generally it pays inadequate attention to issues like cultural diversity and emotional diversity.

(Halstead and Taylor 2000: 60–1)

The educational trend towards making citizenship *explicit* is, however, a response to dramatic changes in the world in which we live, over recent decades. Increased complexity in many aspects of social and cultural, political and educational life has led to educational initiatives like citizenship. Recent international research, for example, on wider factors influencing citizenship education suggests that:

The last two decades have witnessed a fundamental review of the concept of citizenship and what it involves in communities across the world. This review has been brought about by the impact of the rapid pace of change in modern societies in the realms of political, economic and social life and the need to respond to this impact. The pace of change is having significant influence on the nature of relationships in modern society at a number of levels, including within, between and across individuals, community groups, states, nations, regions and economic and political blocs. This period of unprecedented and seemingly relentless change has succeeded in shifting and straining the traditional, stable boundaries of citizenship in many societies. There has been particular pressure on the nature of relationships between differing groups in society as well as those between the individual and the state. The pressure has triggered a fundamental review across societies of the concepts and practices that underpin citizenship.

(Kerr 2003: 9)

A review of citizenship education across countries in response to such dramatic change reveals a common set of issues and challenges that the unprecedented pace of global change was presenting national educational systems (Kerr 2003), including:

- the rapid movement of people within and across national boundaries;
- a growing recognition of the rights of indigenous peoples and minorities;
- the collapse of existing political structures and the fledgeling growth of new ones;
- the changing role and status of women in society;
- the impact of the global economy and changing patterns of work and trade on social, economic and political ties;
- the effects of the revolution in information and communications technologies;
- an increasing global population and the consequences for the environment;
- the emergence of new forms of community and protest.

(Kerr 2003: 9)

Citizenship education, then, is an active – and at present highly transitional – response to these challenges (Gearon 2003b).

The Final Report of the Advisory Group on Citizenship, chaired by Professor Bernard Crick, was published in 1998 and formed the basis for the National Curriculum Citizenship Order that followed a year later (DfEE 1999). Its aims are evangelical in their sense of mission – fundamentally political as much as educational: 'We aim at no less than a change in the political culture of this country both nationally and locally.' Such a vision and purpose is a challenge to the perceived indifference of young people especially to politics, democratic process and active, community involvement. Yet Crick, and much of what followed from Crick, is contentious, disputed in its most basic terms, and, in terms of the mandate for the use of 'we', highly controversial (as well as self-evidently undemocratic). Davies (1999, 2000) has, for instance, identified close to 200 definitions of citizenship in education. In all of this there are many as yet unresolved implications for teachers and policy-makers, as much as for academic researchers. The role of academic researchers – who may themselves be teachers and policy-makers – is not simply to highlight theoretical issues but to present evidence-based assessments of citizenship. Such research can then inform practice – in community involvement, in classrooms and through policy development.

The Crick Report outlines the supposed fourfold benefits of citizenship education:

- for pupils – an entitlement in schools that will empower them to participate in society effectively as active, informed, critical and responsible citizens;
- for teachers – advice and guidance in making existing citizenship provision coherent,

both in intellectual and curriculum terms, as part of stronger, coordinated approaches to citizenship education in schools;
- for schools – a firm base to coordinate existing teaching and activities, to relate positively to the local community and to develop effective citizenship education in the curriculum for all pupils;
- for society – an active and politically-literate citizenry convinced that they can influence government and community affairs at all levels.

Crick's transformative aims represent what McLaughlin (1992, 2000) has characterised as a 'maximal' as opposed to 'minimal' definition of citizenship. Crick represents the citizen as having the potential to participate actively in democratic and political processes in the widest sense (a 'maximal' approach), rather than simply upholding democratic ideals and participating in, say, local and national elections through voting (a 'minimal' approach).

The major curriculum conclusions formulated in Crick are a fourfold framework: 'Aims and Purpose', 'Strands', 'Essential Elements', and 'Learning Outcomes'. The three strands are the most prominent and regularly cited aspects of Crick:

Social and moral responsibility
Children learning from the beginning self-confidence and socially and morally responsible behaviour both in and beyond the classroom, both towards those in authority and towards each other;
Community involvement
Pupils learning about and becoming helpfully involved in the life and concerns of their communities, including learning through community involvement and service to the community;
Political literacy
Pupils learning about and how to make themselves effective in public life through knowledge, skills and values.

Social and moral responsibility, community involvement and political literacy – altered only slightly in terminology – form the bedrock of National Curriculum citizenship which sets out what schools are required to teach under similar headings, expecting pupils to have:

- Knowledge and understanding about becoming informed citizens
- Developing skills of enquiry and communication
- Developing skills of participation and responsible action

(DfEE 1999)

Most research undertaken to date, with some exceptions, has been concerned with terminological issues about the meaning and definition of citizenship in Crick and the implications of the National Curriculum (Heater 1999; Flew 2000; Lawton *et al.* 2000). As citizenship develops from its National Curriculum infancy there are increasing numbers of empirical research studies, and these have recently been summarised by the British Educational Research Association (Gearon 2003a).

Citizenship and religious education: conflict in the curriculum

In one of the only recent studies of international perspectives on citizenship related to issues of religious diversity and religious education, Jackson (2002) contextualises the present debate in the setting of post-Enlightenment challenges to old certainties: of reason as a single or contradictory and competing 'rationalities', the shift towards late or high modernity (Giddens 1998) or postmodern (Lyotard 1984) plurality. But as the theorists debate, 'tangible changes in social, political and economic life make it evident that the traditional idea of the nation-state is being eroded':

> The globalizing tendencies related to massive advances in information and communication technology have enhanced world trade, yet have also reinforced inequalities, especially between countries of the North and South. Multinational companies can be more wealthy than some individual nation-states and are capable of wielding huge power, sometimes against the interests of the poor or causing long-term damage to the environment. Those committed to universal human rights, to the reduction of inequality or to the conservation of the environment (and some of them are religious voices) can find themselves at odds with government policies perceived as promoting a narrow national interest at the expense of the poor or with policies of multinational companies seeming to show scant regard for the long-term future of the planet. In ways such as these, global concerns can have a reciprocal relationship with concerns of particular local groups within countries, affecting individuals' relationships with and views of the nation-state. For example, there are those who would both act as citizens of particular countries and also argue for global governmental structures beyond the nation-state to eradicate poverty, and to exercise constraint over multinational companies. Moreover, there is the issue of nation-states belonging to wider political and economic groupings and of the potential fragmentation of nation-states through devolution.
>
> (Jackson 2002: 3–4)

Religious education in Britain has for too long ignored these historical shifts, as if the traditions can be seen in political isolation.

Many of the well-meaning tendencies of the QCA model syllabuses concerning tolerance and understanding are in part responsible. The search for accommodation can lead to a facile understanding of traditions. Jackson's (1997) interpretive approach avoids this by remaining focused on the philosophical and theological 'essences' of traditions while having an eye on the changing social and historical realities of lived communities. In terms of the diversity of debates about citizenship and plurality in modern/late-/high-/post-modern societies:

Education in citizenship, then, needs to take account of these different but interrelated forms of plurality. There needs to be an informed exploration of the debates about identity and belonging in relation to the nation-state, and also in relation to global and more local issues. These issues are related in a variety of ways, but especially so in 'multicultural' societies where some citizens have transnational links with other family members or co-religionists.

(Jackson 2002: 4)

But what remains unresolved is the kind of forum for religious education where traditions themselves can be challenged. Citizenship as a subject presents such possibilities.

The QCA scheme of work for citizenship presents a religious education link through a unit on conflict. It looks at what conflict is and how it arises; what different religions teach about forgiveness; and the importance of these teachings in resolving conflict. It examines forgiveness through pupils' own examples as well as the examples of reconciliation offered by key historical figures and groups. The unit examines conflict in personal relationships, local communities and the global community. It evaluates the need for understanding, respect and compromise and reflects on contemporary issues. Making a major and welcome development in the political dimension of religious education, the exemplar is worth reproducing here (see pp. 15–21).

This is not the place to rehearse the modern history of religious education when others have already done so more than adequately (Copley 1997, 2000), but religious education in the United Kingdom remains, to all intents and purposes, almost entirely unengaged politically. The QCA unit on conflict is an excellent example of what has been lacking in the subject in its various modern guises since the 1944 Education Act.

Michael Grimmitt's (2000) survey of pedagogies of religious education, for instance, presents the work of 'those who have been responsible for undertaking, with their colleagues, some of the most important and influential research and development work in RE in the UK during the last twenty five years', including, aside from Grimmitt himself, Alan Brown, Trevor Cooling, Clive and Jane Erricker, David Hay, John Hull, Robert Jackson, John Rudge, and Andrew Wright. Here is not the place to review in full this significant pedagogical diversity, but there is a conspicuous absence of a political dimension to most of these approaches. The risk of generalisation is worth taking, especially if it will lead to further debate. So we have anthropological approaches which look at small-scale societies from an ethnographic perspective but neglect macroeconomic and socio-political concerns (Rudge 2000: 88–111; Jackson 2000: 130–52). We have supposedly global approaches to teaching religious tradition which neglect the imperialist missionary enterprises of the past (Brown 2000: 53–69). We have conceptual modes of religious development which fail to identify the mechanism of political power and imposed models of western rationalism which lie behind so many cultural constructions (Cooling 2000: 153–69; Wright 2000: 170–87). And so forth. This is certainly not an attempt to undermine any of the latter contributions to religious education theory or practice. Yet the absence of a significant political consciousness in these approaches to religious education is near self-evident. This is obviously a highly problematic starting point for teaching citizenship through religious education.

QCA citizenship unit on conflict

13 How do we deal with conflict?

About the unit

Schools need to decide which opportunities to develop as explicit citizenship provision. This unit explores conflict and ways of resolving it and is designed to be delivered through citizenship or RE. It looks at what conflict is and how it arises; what different religions teach about forgiveness; and the importance of these teachings in resolving conflict. It examines forgiveness through pupils' own examples as well as the examples of reconciliation offered by key historical figures and groups.

The unit examines conflict in personal relationships, local communities and the global community. It evaluates the need for understanding, respect and compromise and reflects on contemporary issues.

Where the unit fits in

This unit addresses the following aspects of the key stage 3 citizenship programme of study:

Knowledge and understanding about becoming informed citizens

Pupils should be taught about:

1f the work of community-based, national and international voluntary groups

1g the importance of resolving conflict fairly

1i the world as a global community, and the political, economic, environmental and social implications of this, and the role of the European Union, the Commonwealth and the United Nations

Developing skills of enquiry and communication

Pupils should be taught to:

2a think about topical political, spiritual, moral, social and cultural issues, problems and events by analysing information and its sources, including ICT-based sources

2b justify orally and in writing a personal opinion about such issues, problems or events

2c contribute to group and exploratory class discussions, and take part in debates

Developing skills of participation and responsible action

Pupils should be taught to:

3a use their imagination to consider other people's experiences and be able to think about, express and explain views that are not their own.

This unit links with unit 13 'Debating a global issue', unit 11 'Why is it so difficult to keep the peace in the world today?', unit 7 'Local democracy' and unit 8 'Leisure and sport'

This unit also links with many aspects of RE in local agreed syllabuses and with the following units in the RE scheme of work at key stage 3: unit 7B 'What does justice mean to Christians?', unit 8C 'Belief and practice (generic)', unit 9C 'Why do we suffer?', unit 9D 'Why are some places special to religious believers?'.

Expectations

At the end of this unit

most pupils: understand different types of conflict. They understand Christian and other religions' teachings on forgiveness and conflict. They recognise that forgiveness is not always easy and it may be necessary to compromise. They understand that not forgiving may result in further conflict. They know about the major religions' Holy Sites in Jerusalem or other areas of conflict. They describe how some religions share some beliefs and values and ask relevant questions about identity, tradition, conflict and peace. They discuss their opinions of conflict, forgiveness, compromise and reconciliation, and make an informed response.

some pupils have not made so much progress and: understand some aspects of conflict. They know about people and groups of people who work to resolve conflict. They recognise the struggle that some individuals, communities or religions experience in achieving reconciliation and forgiveness. They consider basic questions of respect in Jerusalem or other places of conflict.

some pupils have progressed further and: understand how simple conflict relates to global conflict. They critically evaluate the outcomes of continuing conflict or compromise and reconciliation in places like Jerusalem. They understand political situations, their religious dimensions and the difficulties in resolving them.

Resources

Many groups and organisations produce online resources that are relevant to citizenship. QCA has not printed these website addresses as it recognises that they can and do change, often at short notice. So that we can monitor and maintain a reliable and useful resource, the website addresses of the following organisations can be accessed through the key stage 3 citizenship scheme of work site at www.standards.dfes.gov.uk/schemes

- United Nations High Commissioner for Refugees
- United Nations Association UK
- Religious Tolerance (OCRT) *(promotes tolerance of all faiths)*
- Interfaith *(information on various religious and spiritual organisations)*
- Muscade *(reference point for anyone interested in RE)*
- TAIZE
- Coventry Cathedral
- Community Service Volunteers' online database of voluntary organisations
- Muslim Aid
- Christian Aid
- Amnesty International
- World Council of Churches
- QCA *(for information on RE)*

NB: care should be taken when encouraging pupils to access websites

Literacy and language

References to the Key Stage 3 National Strategy *Framework for teaching English, Years 7, 8 and 9* (NSE) are given in brackets and are indicated in appropriate sections of this unit.

Through the activities in this unit pupils will be able to understand, use and spell correctly words relating to:

- conflict, *eg persecution, dialogue, co-existence, respect, compromise*
- resolution, *eg forgiveness, reconciliation and renewal*
- names of places connected with conflict in the world, *eg Jerusalem, Yad Vashem, Corymeela*

Speaking and listening – through the activities pupils learn to:
- use speculative talk to develop thinking about complex issues (year 7 S&L12, year 8 S&L10, year 9 S&L9)

Writing – through the activities pupils learn to:
- assemble ideas in an appropriate planning format (year 7 Wr2, year 9 Wr2)

Links with other subjects

PSHE: 3h, 3i

LEARNING OBJECTIVES PUPILS SHOULD LEARN:	POSSIBLE TEACHING ACTIVITIES	LEARNING OUTCOMES PUPILS:	POINTS TO NOTE

What do we mean by conflict?

LEARNING OBJECTIVES PUPILS SHOULD LEARN:	POSSIBLE TEACHING ACTIVITIES	LEARNING OUTCOMES PUPILS:	POINTS TO NOTE
• to define conflict and learn about the different types of conflict • to examine different perspectives on conflict and consider why conflicts arise • how conflict affects individuals and communities • to assemble ideas in an appropriate planning format (NSE)	• Ask the pupils, working in pairs or groups, to study newspaper and magazine pictures of conflict between individuals, groups of people or communities. Include young people and parents, bullying situations, violence, arguments between friends, groups threatening one person or another group, and possible racial conflict. What kind of conflict is happening in the picture? What are the people doing? What could have happened before the picture was taken? And after? How does the situation affect those in the picture? Might it affect others who are not in the picture? • Ask pupils to consider other situations of conflict they know about. These could be at school or in the media. Include local, regional, national and international situations. • Build a class list of types of conflicts and ask the pupils to discuss common features. Ask pupils to work in pairs to produce a definition of conflict. • Pupils select one conflict situation and consider how it affects individuals and communities. In groups, they produce a storyboard to show the conflict, its origin and one possible outcome.	• define conflict • identify different kinds of conflict and why they arise • understand how conflict begins and how it affects individuals and communities	• Review with pupils their agreed ground rules at the start of the unit (see *Teacher's guide* and introductory unit 1 'Citizenship – what's it all about?'). • Make pupils aware that this is not a forum for them to air grievances against other pupils. • Control difficult groups by asking pupils to write down points to share with the class one at a time. • This topic may be influenced by media coverage of current world conflicts. Take care not to perpetuate stereotypical views. • The topic may provide a teaching opportunity in resolving conflict in class. • Link with thinking skills: enquiry, reasoning. • Link with NSE: year 7 Wr2, year 9 Wr2.

LEARNING OBJECTIVES PUPILS SHOULD LEARN:	POSSIBLE TEACHING ACTIVITIES	LEARNING OUTCOMES PUPILS:	POINTS TO NOTE
What part does forgiveness play in resolving conflict?			
• about the teachings of Jesus and other key religious figures concerning forgiveness • about forgiveness: that it is not always easy and that it may have a big impact on people • about forgiving and forgetting and the importance of the link between repentance and forgiveness	• Pupils could study the parable of the Unmerciful Servant (Mt18:21–35) and discuss what Jesus was trying to teach. Ask them to write a modern version of this parable, thinking about different possible outcomes. • Ask pupils to consider Jesus forgiving his executioners (Lk23:34). They could watch an extract from the film *Jesus of Nazareth* to help stimulate a discussion about how the people at the crucifixion may have felt and why. • Look at The Lord's Prayer (Lk11:2–4) and consider things that pupils forgive and might like to be forgiven for. • Pupils study the teachings of religious leaders such as Guru Nanak, the Buddha, Muhammad ﷺ and Moses on forgiveness, reconciliation, and how to treat other people. How were these teachings originally taught? How do they influence followers now? Are there any similarities between the religions? What lessons are there for people who are not members of a faith group? How do different religions respect and/or tolerate the views of others? Is fairness always a factor in reconciliation? • Ask pupils to write about forgiveness. They could base it on personal experiences, or on imaginary characters. • Ask pupils to return to the storyboard produced earlier and develop an ending that reflects what they have learnt about forgiveness and reconciliation. In this activity they should illustrate fairness, respect for and tolerance of the views of others.	• understand Jesus' attitude to forgiveness • explain the significance of Jesus' teaching for aspects of life today • understand the teaching of other religious leaders on forgiveness and discuss its significance to aspects of life today • describe how it feels to forgive, or not; or to be forgiven, or not; and explain how difficult this might be for people • respond to issues such as expecting others to forgive us if we will not forgive them; and appreciate what happens if we forgive but do not forget, and how to feel and express real forgiveness • recognise that forgiveness can be difficult and involves empathy with others • respect and tolerate the views of others	• The choice of religions depends on locally agreed syllabus requirements. • There is always a danger of promoting an ideal of a key religious figure that followers do not always live up to. The lesson should include the reasons for this. • There is much opportunity here for reflective work and spiritual development. It may also be appropriate to further develop the theme of forgiving and forgetting.

LEARNING OBJECTIVES PUPILS SHOULD LEARN:	POSSIBLE TEACHING ACTIVITIES	LEARNING OUTCOMES PUPILS:	POINTS TO NOTE
Are forgiveness and conflict resolution possible?			
• about specific situations in which forgiveness and conflict resolution are implemented, eg Coventry, Northern Ireland • some of the values expressed in these situations • about current situations of conflict, and the role of local, national and international groups	• Use the story of Coventry Cathedral and the work for reconciliation following the Second World War to discuss why people thought it necessary to work for peace. • Explore reconciliation stories from Northern Ireland where Protestants and Catholics work together. Pupils could consider the work of the Corymeela Community, the World Council of Churches, local churches and the ecumenical movement. Songs from the musical 'The Beautiful Game' may act as illustrations. • Discuss with the pupils the motivation and idealism behind such initiatives. Use thought bubbles to connect texts and ideals with real events, and balance diagrams where there are tensions to be resolved. • Explore current conflict situations as they arise. Pupils could address the religious and other factors that are involved through debate and speech writing. They consider the work of voluntary organisations and inter-faith groups such as the United Nations and other agencies, eg Christian Aid, Muslim Aid, Amnesty International. • Use flow charts to show a sequence of events that will lead to no forgiveness. Repeat the diagram, this time ending with forgiveness. Discuss with the pupils the differences and the difficulties for those involved.	• describe situations in which people find it difficult to forgive, and explain why • explain that forgiveness and reconciliation may lead to peace, and give examples • realise that not forgiving may lead to a chain of further events involving anger, hatred and escalation of the conflict	• There are many examples of individuals or communities working towards reconciliation. • Refer to the Community Service Volunteers' online database of voluntary organisations (see www.standards.dfes.gov.uk/schemes). • The Coventry Cathedral website includes information about reconciliation resources. • There are also many examples of forgiveness in action, eg Gordon Wilson in Northern Ireland. • Link with thinking skills: enquiry, reasoning.

LEARNING OBJECTIVES
PUPILS SHOULD LEARN:
POSSIBLE TEACHING ACTIVITIES
LEARNING OUTCOMES
PUPILS:
POINTS TO NOTE

A contemporary situation – Jerusalem: conflict or reconciliation?

LEARNING OBJECTIVES PUPILS SHOULD LEARN:	POSSIBLE TEACHING ACTIVITIES	LEARNING OUTCOMES PUPILS:	POINTS TO NOTE
• that Jerusalem is important to Jews, Christians and Muslims • to understand why Jerusalem is a place of conflict, in a region of conflict • about examples of conflict, coexistence, dialogue and harmony in Jerusalem which have implications elsewhere, including in their own communities • to use speculative talk to develop thinking about complex issues (NSE)	• Explore the reasons for the current situation in Jerusalem. Ask pupils to draw a map of the Walled City of Jerusalem showing the major sites for each religion. Point out how each is close to, or part of, another's traditional area. • Use textbooks, tour guides and videos to explore the historical and religious traditions of the sites. Include the Dome of the Rock; Western Wall; Via Dolorosa; Yad Vashem; and Church of the Holy Sepulchre. • In groups, pupils discuss the possibility of a shared holy city. Pupils' ideas could form part of a project about their opinions and hopes for the future in Jerusalem. • Carry out a similar exercise for other forms of conflict, including within pupils' own communities (see next topic).	• understand why there is conflict in and around Jerusalem • describe the points of view of people who live there and are involved in the conflict • produce an informed summary of their own views and opinions • appreciate why reconciliation is difficult but necessary, and realise the need for dialogue and possible need for compromise	• Link with RE: unit 9D 'Why are some places special to religious believers?'. This unit includes more details of voluntary groups and resources. • Link with ICT: use ICT to research the major sites. • Focus on Yad Vashem and what this represents. • The ways in which the media interpret events can be useful for discussions about media bias. • A similar approach could be taken to other well-known places of conflict such as sites in India, and pupils' local communities where there may be conflict between members of different groups. • Link with thinking skills: evaluation. • Link with NSE: year 7 S&L12, year 8 S&L10, year 9 S&L9.

LEARNING OBJECTIVES
PUPILS SHOULD LEARN:

POSSIBLE TEACHING ACTIVITIES

LEARNING OUTCOMES
PUPILS:

POINTS TO NOTE

How can conflict be resolved?

LEARNING OBJECTIVES PUPILS SHOULD LEARN:	POSSIBLE TEACHING ACTIVITIES	LEARNING OUTCOMES PUPILS:	POINTS TO NOTE
• to apply the lessons about conflict to their own communities • how coexistence, peace and harmony and the need for dialogue may be necessary locally and nationally • to consider their own attitudes to conflict resolution • to put into practice their ideas for conflict resolution	• Review what the class has learnt about conflict and conflict resolution. Ask pupils to identify the factors they think need to be present for a peaceful end to conflict. Can they apply these factors or actions to a conflict situation they know about? (This could be a personal, school or community conflict.) They could contact the local Standing Advisory Council for RE (SACRE) and local inter-faith groups to discuss community issues that involve different faith groups. • Discuss symbols of peace and their importance, *eg the Dove of Peace*. Let pupils design their own symbol for reconciliation. • Ask pupils to analyse, in pairs, some dilemmas involving forgiveness and dialogue. Encourage them to think of case studies and stories, whether they are from television programmes or are real situations. Should they forgive? If so, why, when and how? What happens if they do not forgive? How would they start dialogue and reconciliation? Offer feedback to the whole class. • Pupils could prepare a Peace Charter for personal, school or community situations. Discuss how they would publish and implement it. How would they deal with conflict at school?	• identify common features of conflict resolution in different religions • explain the need for reconciliation and dialogue in their own lives • understand the need for principles and compromise: that 'fair' may not mean 'getting our own way' • are aware of, and respond to, contemporary situations in their communities	• Stress the complexity of these issues – there is a danger of over-simplifying complex local, national and international issues. • A safe environment and sensitive handling are necessary if teacher and pupils are to consider conflict in their own lives. There is information in the *Teacher's guide* about dealing with controversial and sensitive issues. • These activities can apply to school conflict situations in the context of the school behaviour policy. • It may be important to involve local and community leaders if there are contentious community issues. • Link with thinking skills: creative thinking.

For the moment, though, the point is plain. The present dissociation of religious education from political reality is a weak starting point for a subject hoping to make its claim to contribute to citizenship, and it is a view shared by some authoritative voices, such as John Keast writing for a professional audience in a special 'Citizenship and RE' edition of *RE Today*:

> RE, as well as other humanities subjects, has a potentially important role to play in its links with citizenship. The importance of values and beliefs for RE is obvious, yet they are also implicit in citizenship. What kind of society do we want? Why? In RE pupils learn about the beliefs and traditions which underpin our sense of moral authority and responsibility. How will they be applied in citizenship? It is possible to make connections of other kinds with other subjects, especially history, geography and economics which provide vital knowledge and understanding as the background and context to political decision making, legal and government institutions, economic development and its impact on the environment.
>
> (Keast 2000: 32)

This notion, fairly explicit here – that 'it is possible to make connections of other kinds with other subjects, especially history, geography and economics which provide vital knowledge and understanding as the background and context to political decision making, legal and government institutions, economic development and its impact on the environment' – implies that religious education has a somewhat 'softer' role. The rejection is based on empirical grounds of religion's increasing influence on and importance in global governance, even before terror in the name of Islam in the aftermath of September 11 (Casanova 1994; Haynes 1998, 2000). Wright (2000) has consistently tried to increase the critical realist dimension of religious education but this takes us no further. In fact, the critical realist approach with its emphasis upon a disembodied rational approach to analysis and critical assessment further decontextualises the subject into an ahistorical, philosophical vacuum where theology and religion can be debated, their ideas balanced medieval-like, little advance on the discussion about how many angels might fit on the top of a pin-head. (Although, of course, this idea of how many angels might fit on a pin-head can be held up to ridicule, it is likely that even medieval theologians had a sense of humour.)

The idea that religion has nothing to do with 'political decision making, legal and government institutions, economic development and its impact on the environment' is as strange as religious education's self-evident neglect of these realities. (The QCA unit on conflict marks a new and important shift in religious education's political consciousness.) Religious studies as a discipline is, after all, a multitude of disciplines: anthropology, history, literary criticism, linguistics, psychology, sociology, and, of course, theology. Religious educators are polymaths, or many are, and those that are not need to become so. So:

> The relationship that RE forges with these new areas needs to be a positive one. They can each complement the others very well in curriculum theory, but in

practice competition for time and resources could be fierce. Is citizenship a threat to RE? Not if handled sensibly from position of confidence in the distinctive and positive role RE has in the curriculum. Whatever some may say, beliefs, values and practices cannot be ignored, nor their study suppressed, without distorting the nature of education. Citizenship actually requires such study if it is to be effective in schools.

(Keast 2000: 32)

Yet religious education is, or should be, more than about beliefs and values. It has no choice if it is make more than a token contribution to citizenship. And much of the bemusement of religious educators at the practicalities of making a contribution results from the fact that many have not been trained to examine their subject from such perspectives. Admittedly, such an assertion is anecdotal. From an overview of pre- and post-1999 citizenship research, we saw that religion does not feature very much in any aspect of discussions of citizenship in education, with some notable exceptions (Jackson 2002).

Box 1.2 takes some of the elements of the citizenship order and plots some possible religious education links. It is not an exhaustive list of possibilities. The teacher may add more, taking the list as a baseline for ideas and curriculum development. What it begins is an attempt at linking broad, macro-level considerations with the day-to-day curriculum, a matter now of practical urgency.

Box 1.2
Citizenship at key stage 3

Teaching should ensure that knowledge and understanding about becoming informed citizens are acquired and applied when developing skills of enquiry and communication, and participation and responsible action.

Knowledge and understanding about becoming informed citizens

1   Pupils should be taught about:

a   the legal and human rights and responsibilities underpinning society and how they relate to citizens, including the role and operation of the criminal and civil justice systems

POSSIBLE RELIGIOUS EDUCATION LINKS: religion and human rights – asylum, death penalty, freedom of religion, belief and expression, genocide, the rights of women, children and indigenous peoples; punishments for infringements of human rights, including the International Criminal Court, and the role of religious persons – victims and perpetrators – in atrocities, conflicts between civil-state law and religious law.

b   the origins and implications of the diverse national, regional, religious and ethnic identities in the United Kingdom and the need for mutual respect and understanding

continued

POSSIBLE RELIGIOUS EDUCATION LINKS: the range of religious belief and practice of Christianity and the other principal religions in Great Britain; traditions beyond the six major world religious traditions, including, internationally, indigenous and tribal peoples; how powerful and numerically superior religious traditions have infringed the rights of religious and other minorities.

c   the work of parliament, the government and the courts in making and shaping the law

POSSIBLE RELIGIOUS EDUCATION LINKS: religion and the state, historically and today; in Britain the monarch as 'Defender of the Faith' and the challenges of a religiously diverse society; monarch as 'Defender of all Faiths'?

d   the importance of playing an active part in democratic and electoral processes

POSSIBLE RELIGIOUS EDUCATION LINKS: religion and democracy, authority structures within religious traditions as modelled on democratic or authoritarian/autocratic structures; relationship of religious traditions with the state, including official or state religions.

e   how the economy functions, including the role of business and financial services

POSSIBLE RELIGIOUS EDUCATION LINKS: development education through religious and other aid/development agencies such as CAFOD, Christian Aid, OXFAM, especially initiatives such as Fair Trade, Jewish Aid, World Jewish Relief, Muslim Aid; social teaching of religious traditions.

f   the opportunities for individuals and voluntary groups to bring about social change locally, nationally, in Europe and internationally

POSSIBLE RELIGIOUS EDUCATION LINKS: development education through religious and other aid/development agencies such as CAFOD, Christian Aid, OXFAM, especially initiatives such as Fair Trade, Jewish Aid, World Jewish Relief, Muslim Aid; social teaching of religious traditions.

g   the importance of a free press, and the media's role in society, including the internet, in providing information and affecting opinion

POSSIBLE RELIGIOUS EDUCATION LINKS: freedom of expression, religion and the media, religious repression and censorship of artists and writers – historically and today.

h   Rights and responsibilities of consumers, employers and employees

POSSIBLE RELIGIOUS EDUCATION LINKS: development education through religious and other aid/development agencies such as CAFOD, Christian Aid, OXFAM, especially initiatives such as Fair Trade, and development/humanitarian organisations from a range of religious traditions, again such as Jewish Aid, World Jewish Relief, Muslim Aid.

i   The United Kingdom's relations in Europe, including the European Union, and relations with the Commonwealth and the United Nations

POSSIBLE RELIGIOUS EDUCATION LINKS: immigration and minorities, the UN Special

continued

Rapporteur on Religion and Belief, religious diversity in the Commonwealth, religion and the history of empire and colonialism, international issues of religious freedom.

j   the wider issues and challenges of global interdependence and responsibility, including sustainable development and Local Agenda 21

POSSIBLE RELIGIOUS EDUCATION LINKS: religion and the environment, stewardship and dominion, development education through religious and other aid/development agencies such as CAFOD, Christian Aid, OXFAM and environmental organisations such as Friends of the Earth, Greenpeace and WWF.

Developing skills of enquiry and communication

2   Pupils should be taught to:
a   research a topical political, spiritual, moral, social or cultural issue, problem or event by analysing information from different sources, including ICT-based sources, showing an awareness of the use and abuse of statistics
b   express, justify and defend orally and in writing a personal opinion about such issues, problems or events
c   contribute to group and exploratory class discussions, and take part in formal debates

POSSIBLE RELIGIOUS EDUCATION LINKS: explore the range of internet sources for any or all of the issues in the last section; project work, surveys, class debates, written assignments; issued-base focus on secular state and religious perspectives on the issues listed in part 1, a–j.

Developing skills of participation and responsible action

3   Pupils should be taught to:
a   use their imagination to consider other people's experiences and be able to think about, express, explain and critically evaluate views that are not their own
b   negotiate, decide and take part responsibly in school- and community-based activities
c   reflect on the process of participating

POSSIBLE RELIGIOUS EDUCATION LINKS: critically explore the dissonance between universal human rights in the UN system and possible clashes with particular cultural and especially religious worldviews and ethical systems; explore possibilities for placements with or visits to leading religious/secular NGOs, local charities or religious communities, exploring convergence of rights thinking between the religious and the secular; evaluation of work-based placement, for example, in a leading NGO, local charity or religious com- munity; exploring further, on the basis of experience, the convergence of rights thinking between the religious and the secular.

We might close this chapter by seeing how some of these links refer to issues of pressing historical urgency and not simply niceties of the curriculum, and do so in a seemingly roundabout way by looking at the challenges raised by the encounter of two Viennese-born philosophers.

The Open Society and Its Enemies

The one and only time that the two philosophers, Ludwig Wittgenstein and Karl Popper, met was in a room in Cambridge just after the Second World War, on 25 October 1946. The best-selling book that detailed their meeting was called *Wittgenstein's Poker* written by David Edmonds and John Eidinow. The title arose from the contested story of Wittgenstein's reaction to Popper's talk when, it is alleged, Wittgenstein – and, by some accounts, threateningly – raised a poker at the visiting lecturer, Karl Popper. Edmonds and Eidinow cleverly present the confrontation as one between two philosophies.

Wittgenstein was a philosopher who regarded philosophy itself as a matter of eliminating confusion over language. He decried the notion that there were philosophical problems at all. To Wittgenstein philosophical problems were simply 'puzzles', a matter of resolving difficulties over linguistic expression. Philosophy in this case was a matter of being clear about the language we use to resolve such puzzles. Although both philosophers came from Vienna, Popper had closer experience of totalitarianism – for one, Popper was, in contrast to the wealthy Wittgenstein already living in England and who could buy his family out of Austria, unprotected from the developing threats of Nazi totalitarianism. From such a life world, Popper could not accept that philosophy was simply a matter of resolving 'puzzles'. To Popper philosophical problems not only existed but philosophy had a duty to present practical as well as theoretical resolutions not only in the world of ideas but in the public domains of politics, economics and society at large. Edmonds and Eidinow present an assessment of the lasting influence of the two positions and ultimately suggest that Wittgenstein's philosophy has had a more enduring appeal. I want to present the case that this may be so in philosophy but – in a post-September 11 world – Popper may have unexpected relevance to religious education.

Foremost a philosopher who extolled the principle that scientific truths are those for which empirical falsification can be offered, Popper extended this trial and error methodology to his political philosophy. Popper's demonstration of the practical nature of philosophy was rooted in his observations of real human suffering under the Nazis in his native Austria. (Interestingly, both Popper and Wittgenstein were schoolteachers, but for varying reasons – Popper by necessity, and Wittgenstein for reasons more difficult to fathom.) Popper's *The Open Society and Its Enemies* was fundamentally an attack upon the social, political factors – such as blind belief in the progress of history – that lead to totalitarianism.

Amongst Popper's most controversial targets was the ancient Greek philosopher Plato whose famous political thinking in *The Republic* tolerated the existence of slavery. *The Open Society* was also an attack on the modern political philosophies which also tolerated slavery under different forms – and here Popper attacked the historical determinism of Marx. In political practice – and remember Popper published *The Open Society* almost exactly mid-way through the twentieth century – the natural target for Popper was communist totalitarianism as well as Nazi tyranny. In later decades this would make Popper Margaret Thatcher's favourite philosopher. In the most non-technical of terms, Popper's great idea in political thought was that totalitarianism and all that it entailed in terms of human (physical and mental) enslavement was always a possibility. Democracy was not an automatic given for society. The price of democracy is eternal vigilance. As Edmunds and Eidinow suggest:

> Popper's idea that progress comes through trial and error was one of the truly great ideas of the twentieth century and, like many truly great ideas, it had the mark of utter simplicity. Error was always possible: a 'truth' was never certain. Just as the possibility of falsification is what distinguishes true science from pseudo-science, so the need to test, probe and scrutinise is what makes the open society essential if political advances are to be made. Popper's insight was to recognize that democracy should be viewed merely as a luxury, something a country can afford only once it has reached a certain stage of development. Rather, democracy is a prerequisite to progress.
>
> (Edmonds and Eidinow 2001: 190)

Popper's notion of democracy was open and participatory, not simply about how we elect leaders. Hitler was, after all, elected by democratic principles.

In his philosophical autobiography, *Unended Quest*, Popper comments:

> In [*The Open Society*] I proposed replacing the Platonic question, 'Who shall rule?' with a radically different one: 'How can we draw up the constitution in such a way that we are able to get rid of the government without bloodshed?' The question places the stress not on the mode of *electing* a government but on the possibility of *removing* it.
>
> (cited in Edmonds and Eidinow 2001: 190)

Popper was not alone in thinking that philosophy was more than simply about resolving problems about language. Wittgenstein's one-time ally at Cambridge, Bertrand Russell, had also written on abstract philosophical issues of mathematics, language and logic – but he was also passionately involved in a number of political struggles. In the post-war period, these political efforts were increasingly focused on the nuclear threat. Such apocalyptic concerns were integral to the rise of Soviet power in the context of an economically weak if militarily victorious Europe:

> Although the war was over, the future of Europe looked bleak. Industry lay in ruins, basic necessities were in short supply, communist parties were flourishing in some western democracies, the Soviets were strengthening their grip in eastern Europe and developing the bomb. These developments presented the West with immediate threats to its democratic future. Meanwhile, Popper and Russell frustratedly watched Wittgenstein persuade a generation of new philosophers that philosophy was solely, as they saw, trifling with language. It was essential for the future of philosophy that this deception should be exposed.
>
> (Edmonds and Eidinow 2001: 191)

At present (2002), the European Union has just agreed an expansion of member nations to include many of those formally separated by the Cold War, even after the fall of the

Berlin Wall and the Soviet Union. The United States of America with its allies is engaged in a fundamentalist-inspired 'war against terror'. Committed to its laudable ideals of tolerance and understanding, the silence of religious education on matters of real controversy here is not encouraging. It simply lacks the language at present to express dissent. In a way this is where citizenship comes in useful. International legal and other norms present interesting and real challenges to religious traditions in real political situations.

Edmonds and Eidinow's summary of the differing reputations of Wittgenstein and Popper is instructive. Unfavourably contrasting the influence of Wittgenstein (unchallenged genius) and (influential in his time) Popper, the authors – publishing in 2001 but writing from a pre-September 11 perspective – suggest of the latter:

> In new democracies and closed societies, *The Open Society* retains its freshness and relevance. It has now been translated into over thirty languages, and further editions are constantly planned. But in Britain and America, Popper is slowly being dropped from university syllabuses; his name is fading, if not yet forgotten. This, admittedly, is a penalty of success rather than the price of failure. Many of the political ideas which in 1946 seemed so radical and were so important have become received wisdom. The attacks on dogma and historical inevitability, the stress on tolerance and humility – these today are beyond challenge and so debate. *If a resurgence of communism, fascism, aggressive nationalism or religious fundamentalism once again threatened the international order based on the open society, then Popper's works would have to be reopened and their arguments relearned.*
>
> (Edmonds and Eidinow 2001: 250–1, emphasis added)

Religious education has for too long rested on the assumption that religion is to be treated out of context of the political ramifications of its effects in the world – aside, that is, from where religious education touches on seemingly 'soft' 'personal and social' issues; no one, for instance, can disagree about the need to do something about the environment. But the ground is less certain when we are talking about religious fundamentalism and intolerance or the religious denial of fundamental human rights.

Magee, amongst the most authoritative critics of Popper, presents the following appraisal:

> The maximum possible tolerance or freedom is an optimum, not an absolute, for it has to be restricted if it is to exist at all. The government intervention which alone can guarantee it is a dangerous weapon: without it, or with too little, freedom dies; but with too much of it freedom dies also. We are brought to the inescapability of control – which must mean, if it is to be effective, removability – of government by the governed as the *sine qua non* of democracy. This, however, though necessary, is not sufficient. It does not guarantee the preservation of freedom, for nothing can: the price of freedom is eternal vigilance.
>
> (Magee 1985: 81)

The freedoms that by the turn of the third millennium were being taken for granted in a post-Cold War world were seemingly so certain in their liberal democratic assumptions that many assumed this was the end of history (Fukuyama 1992). September 11, 2001 put an end to this certainty; and the threat came, however misguidedly, in the name of religion.

The present juncture for religious education and citizenship is thus a timely one. In curriculum terms, religious education – the subject which might have been thought to have best provided answers to such crisis – sank back into denial. The denial came in the disavowal that this crisis had anything to do with religion in its 'pristine' state. What was conducted in the name of Islam was not really Islam. It is only natural for a tradition to distance itself from the worst manifestations of its historical realities. But it is like saying that the Inquisition had nothing to do with Roman Catholicism. Or that murder committed through the Reformation and counter-Reformation in the sixteenth century had nothing to do with 'true' Christianity. This of course is not to say that all such atrocities are not terribly misguided interpretations of, say, Islam or Christianity. But what religious educators arguably need to confront more fully is why devotees of a particular faith use the name of faith to commit atrocity. Religion, like politics, is messy. While tolerance and understanding are as essential to democracies as they are to religious education, hiding behind vacuous notions of tolerance and understanding *without* any attempt to assess the educational limits of tolerance, understanding and acceptance will not take us very far; and certainly will be inadequate for teaching citizenship through religious education.

Like political systems, religions build upon visions of utopia: the best possible states of social being for human beings. Religions differ from political systems, however, in the obvious sense of adding to models of the human world (usually seen as imperfect) models of hope for a perfect world beyond this material one. Religions, like political systems, also tend to place human beings in a privileged position. If, given what we have come to understand about cosmology, this is no longer a place at the centre of the universe, then it is certainly at the pinnacle of creation/evolution. Political systems, like religious systems, build upon visions of the best possible social state. Yet this best possible state of being has never been realised. There is more evidence for dystopia than utopia. The twentieth century itself is a testimony to failure of many political visions of utopia, including fascism and communism. But while many have disregarded the religious systems that once upheld repressive political regimes in history (and most religions have these exploitative, mercenary dimensions somewhere in their history), the religious traditions themselves are still around today. If we had a political system guilty of atrocity and carnage on a mass scale with repressive laws, would the political system still be in place? Some would say yes. And certainly the question of historical inheritance and present survival is an interesting and important question.

Conclusion

If the freedom and tolerance of diversity so treasured by religious educators are to be maintained, those who teach citizenship and religious education need to possess the necessary skills to deal with threats to such freedom and tolerance, particularly when such threats come from religious traditions themselves. The remainder of the chapters in this section will draw out some of these themes about conflict and conflict resolution, and the curriculum as mirror to the world, especially a world so plural and diverse in its interpretations of social and cultural, political and economic, as well as existential and theological order. Box 1.3 presents some areas for questioning, discussing and researching issues raised by this chapter. And to close these reflections, we might recall the central implication from Popper's *Open Society and Its Enemies*: that the price of freedom is eternal vigilance. With eyes closed to the harsh realities of political history, it is an eternal vigilance that religious education has for too long neglected.

Box 1.3
Human rights and religious education: question, discuss, research

Question and discuss

1   Do some religions pose a threat to democracy?
2   Why are some religious traditions the target of more prejudice than others?
3   Are religions that tend towards being political more likely to be targets for prejudice?
4   Does religious education have a problem which criticising religious traditions, both in terms of their historical record and contemporary claims?
5   If violence and terrorist activity are claimed in the name of religion, can the tradition in question claim, 'This is not truly . . . '?
6   Is Popper's idea of an open society worth protecting and at what cost?
7   Is democracy a western political concept imposed on the rest of the world without respect for different forms of government?
8   How far should religion be politically involved? Can religion be apolitical?
9   Should religious educators be more politically informed?

Research

10 Review the QCA website at www.qca.gov.uk and links to both citizenship and religious education. Is citizenship a threat to religious education? Can the two make contributions to each other's curriculum?

Chapter 2

The politics of hell on earth
Human rights and religious education

Introduction

We have suggested so far that religious education needs to take more account of the political implications of teaching and learning, especially in the representation of religious traditions. It is in those aspects of political and religious life where the greatest ideals are present that realities often fall shortest. In politics, as in education, the utopian agenda for religious education is often confronted with the global and too often dystopian realities of cultural conflict. And there is no area of political life or international relations more contested than the universality of human rights – in their justification, in their use and abuse, in their manipulation for self-interested ends, in their clearly inequitable distribution; nor any area where religious traditions are more set to challenge international standards with their own culturally determined traditions.

The politics of hell on earth

With advanced technologies of communication, we are more aware today of the wrongs in the world. But even with rudimentary news footage – say the Pathé news of the Second World War period, broadcast to cinema audiences – the horror of the liberation of Nazi death camps was as apparent as it would be with more advanced technology. Media today speeds our access to the horror but it does not lessen it.

Yet we inhabit a world more crowded with human beings than ever and where we are more aware of our neighbours – who has what, who does not. The apparent proximity of our neighbours around the world is often given the over-used title of globalisation. In this world, nation-states are not so easily able to wander across continents and colonise as openly, even if newer, subtler forms of imperialism permit multinationals to do this from offices in Paris or London or New York.

We are thus in an era where we have a postcolonial mentality. We do not generally think that crude empires – where the sun never sets – would be something of which politicians and rulers could now be proud. (Postcolonial theory is a frame of criticism that allows us to think and to clarify power relations within and between religions and cultures as well as between nations and states. Like any tool of criticism it has its limitations (Gearon 2000).) Yet since religion has been so embroiled in empire through missionary activity and since the decline of empire has brought to the shores of Great Britain the religious and cultural diversity which characterises its society today, this postcolonial context – a period beginning in earnest after the Second World War – is critical for our understanding of the introduction of citizenship. Yet, the investigation with which we are presently engaged – how do we approach citizenship through religious education – is very much open in terms of its future, just as it needs to be historically grounded in the past. We begin in an emergent, postcolonial and post-Second World War setting with the self-contradictory inhumanity of human beings, and what for many is the politics of hell on earth.

Human rights, human wrongs

Box 2.1 presents an outline of the Charter of the United Nations signed in San Francisco in 1945. The dates are not insignificant. By 26 June 1945 victory over Nazi tyranny had been gained in Europe. But the war in the East had not yet been won. For all the Charter's talk of peace, the date of the signing of the Charter was a matter of weeks before the bombing of Nagasaki and Hiroshima. Yet, for all its failings as an organisation, the Charter of the United Nations was signed by a world weary of two genuinely global conflicts that had seen the death of millions of soldiers and the beginnings of new forms of war where non-military targets increased exponentially (Ryan 2000). Not only had the atomic bomb dropped on those two Japanese cities changed the face of modern conflict – a threat which even after the end of the Cold War the world still lives with in fear of 'rogue' states and international terrorists gaining such weapons – but the balance had shifted, especially in the Second World War, to the death of civilians. Allied and Axis powers both targeted cities of civilian populations during the Second World War. And in the Holocaust the hopes that modernity and the machine age would lessen the burden of men and women and obviate the need for hard labour turned into a hard lesson in mass death when industrialised processes were used to eliminate the maximum number of people with the maximum efficiency.

The Charter of the United Nations sets out, then, the basic principles of goodwill and co-operation as a basis on which international legal standards have developed in the 'UN era'. A prime question for religious educators to ask is, 'What is there in the Charter of the United Nations that any religious tradition could object to?' The question is as open and genuine as it is rhetorical.

The basic international human rights are contained in the International Bill of Human Rights. This International Bill of Human Rights is really *five* documents consisting of:

- Universal Declaration of Human Rights (10 December 1948)
- International Covenant on Economic, Social and Cultural Rights (16 December 1966, into effect 3 January 1976)
- International Covenant on Civil and Political Rights (16 December 1966, into effect 23 March 1976)
- Optional Protocol to the International Covenant on Civil and Political Rights (16 December 1966, into effect 23 March 1976)

Box 2.1

The Charter of the United Nations

The Charter of the United Nations was signed on 26 June 1945, in San Francisco, at the conclusion of the United Nations Conference on International Organization, and came into force on 24 October 1945.

PREAMBLE

WE THE PEOPLES OF THE UNITED NATIONS DETERMINED
*   to save succeeding generations from the scourge of war, which twice in our lifetime has brought untold sorrow to mankind, and
*   to reaffirm faith in fundamental human rights, in the dignity and worth of the human person, in the equal rights of men and women and of nations large and small, and
*   to establish conditions under which justice and respect for the obligations arising from treaties and other sources of international law can be maintained, and
*   to promote social progress and better standards of life in larger freedom
AND FOR THESE ENDS
*   to practise tolerance and live together in peace with one another as good neighbours, and
*   to unite our strength to maintain international peace and security, and
*   to ensure, by the acceptance of principles, and the institution of methods, that armed force shall not be used, save in the common interest, and
*   to employ international machinery for the promotion of the economic and social advancement of all peoples,
HAVE RESOLVED TO COMBINE OUR EFFORTS TO ACCOMPLISH THESE AIMS
Accordingly, our respective Governments, through representatives assembled in the city of San Francisco, who have exhibited their full powers found to be in good and due form, have agreed to the present Charter of the United Nations and do hereby establish an international organization to be known as the United Nations.

CHAPTER I deals with **PURPOSES AND PRINCIPLES**.
Thus Article 1 states, 'The purposes of the United Nations are:
1. To maintain international peace and security, and to that end: to take effective collective measures for the prevention and removal of threats to the peace, and for the suppression of acts of aggression or other breaches of the peace, and to bring about by peaceful means, and in conformity with the principles of justice and international law, adjustment or settlement of international disputes or situations which might lead to a breach of the peace:
2. To develop friendly relations among nations based on respect for the principle of equal rights and self-determination of peoples, and to take other appropriate measures to strengthen universal peace;
3. To achieve international co-operation in solving international problems of an economic, social, cultural, or humanitarian character, and in promoting and encouraging respect for human rights and fundamental freedoms for all without distinction as to race, sex, language, or religion, and

continued

4. To be a centre for harmonizing the actions of nations in the attainment of these common ends.'

CHAPTER II deals with **MEMBERSHIP** of the United Nations.
Thus **Article 4** states that 'Membership in the United Nations is open to all peace-loving states which accept the obligations contained in the present Charter and, in the judgment of the Organization, are able and willing to carry out these obligations.

CHAPTER III deals with **ORGANS** of the United Nations.
Thus, **Article 7** states that,
'1. There are established as the principal organs of the United Nations:
General Assembly
Security Council
Economic and Social Council
Trusteeship Council
International Court of Justice
A Secretariat
2. Such subsidiary organs as may be found necessary may be established in accordance with the present Charter.'

For a full text of the Charter, follow links at www.un.org

- Second Optional Protocol to the International Covenant on Civil and Political Rights, aiming at the abolition of the death penalty (15 December 1989)

For the text and context of all these follow links on the website of the UN High Commissioner for Human Rights (UNHCHR) at www.unhchr.org or links through the UN homepage at www.un.org (UN 2002a, 2002b, 2002e, 2002h, 2002i, 2002m, 2002r, 2002s, 2002w).

Historians of the UN as well as legal scholars of human rights have, however, been critical of the failings of the international community. Some have been so extreme as to argue that the growth of human rights amounts to nothing more than a self-serving industry of lawyers and politicians and power-seeking non-government organisations (Sellar 2002). Because of the concise manner in which human rights discourse has been used to serve personal or political ambition or ironically even as a tool of oppression, Mansell (1999) highlights some of the most abused aspects of human rights discourse since the 1948 UN Universal Declaration of Human Rights:

A study of the discourse of human rights since the Second World War suggests that the rhetoric of human rights has been determined most clearly by the propaganda value it represented:
- The difference in the sort of human rights different states proclaimed was dictated by the political ideology of each state.

- International institutions with power tend to reflect the interests of powerful states.
- International financial institutions have, by their operation, made the protection of economic rights almost impossible for poor states.
- The economic interests of wealthy states have led indirectly but regularly to human rights abuse whether, for instance, through the export of tobacco, the export of pesticides or the export of subsidised food.
- The aftermath of colonialism continues to bedevil colonial peoples in their attempts to promote and secure self-determination.
- Finally, regardless of proclaimed international standards on human rights, there are some states which may regularly, persistently and blatantly ignore world opinion if their strategic or emotional importance is exceptional.

(Mansell 1999: 57)

This does not present human rights with much of a track record in terms of achieving the equitable state of affairs envisaged by the UN Charter.

Yet the UN is aware of its failings, of how far short its ideals fall from historical and contemporary reality. The 1993 World Conference on Human Rights resulted in the Vienna Plan of Action. Priorities for the global implementation of human rights were listed and, as with the majority of recent UN world conferences, a five-year review was planned. The United Nations Commissioner for Human Rights concludes the Vienna + 5 review in a final paragraph as follows:

> The international community must conclude that five years after Vienna, a wide gap continues to exist between the promise of human rights and their reality in the lives of people throughout the world. At the beginning of the twenty-first century, making all human rights a reality for all remains not only our fundamental challenge but our solemn responsibility.

(UN 1998)

For all this, on 10 December 1948 the General Assembly of the United Nations adopted and proclaimed the Universal Declaration of Human Rights and it remains a benchmark statement of human ideals in a world so often divided by rival ideologies and worldviews. Short on philosophical grounding but high on rhetoric (Forsythe 2000), only the non-inclusive language of the 1948 Preamble to the Universal Declaration weakens the impact of the statement:

> Whereas recognition of the inherent dignity and of the equal and inalienable rights of all members of the human family is the foundation of freedom, justice and peace in the world,
> Whereas disregard and contempt for human rights have resulted in barbarous acts which have outraged the conscience of [humankind] . . .
> Whereas it is essential, if [humanity] is not to be compelled to have recourse, as a last resort, to rebellion against tyranny and oppression, that human rights should be protected by the rule of law . . .

Now, therefore THE GENERAL ASSEMBLY proclaims THIS UNIVERSAL DECLARATION OF HUMAN RIGHTS as a common standard of achievement for all peoples and all nations, to the end that every individual and every organ of society, keeping this Declaration constantly in mind, shall strive by teaching and education. Following this historic act the Assembly called upon all Member countries to publicize the text of the Declaration and 'to cause it to be *disseminated, displayed, read and expounded principally in schools and other educational institutions*, without distinction based on the political status of countries or territories'.

(emphasis added)

Educators (including religious educators) should ask to what extent they have themselves been to blame for a neglect of the historical context and the motivation behind the thirty articles of the Declaration, here represented in abbreviated form in Box 2.2.

Box 2.2
UN Universal Declaration of Human Rights

Article I
All human beings are born free and equal in dignity and rights.

Article 2
Everyone is entitled to all the rights and freedoms set forth in this Declaration, without distinction of any kind, such as race, colour, sex, language, religion, political or other opinion, national or social origin, property, birth or other status.

Article 3
Everyone has the right to life, liberty and security of person.

Article 4
No one shall be held in slavery or servitude; slavery and the slave trade shall be prohibited in all their forms.

Article 5
No one shall be subjected to torture or to cruel, inhuman or degrading treatment or punishment.

Article 6
Everyone has the right to recognition everywhere as a person before the law.

Article 7
All are equal before the law and are entitled without any discrimination to equal protection of the law.

Article 8
Everyone has the right to an effective remedy by the competent national tribunals for acts violating the fundamental rights.

continued

Article 9
No one shall be subjected to arbitrary arrest, detention or exile.

Article 10
Everyone is entitled in full equality to a fair and public hearing by an independent and impartial tribunal.

Article 11
Everyone charged with a penal offence has the right to be presumed innocent until proved guilty according to law in a public trial.

Article 12
No one shall be subjected to arbitrary interference with privacy, family, home or correspondence.

Article 13
Everyone has the right to freedom of movement and residence within the borders of each state.

Article 14
Everyone has the right to seek and to enjoy in other countries asylum from persecution.

Article 15
Everyone has the right to a nationality.

Article 16
Men and women of full age, without any limitation due to race, nationality or religion, have the right to marry and to found a family.

Article 17
Everyone has the right to own property alone as well as in association with others.

Article 18
Everyone has the right to freedom of thought, conscience and religion.

Article 19
Everyone has the right to freedom of opinion and expression.

Article 20
Everyone has the right to freedom of peaceful assembly and association.

Article 21
Everyone has the right to take part in the government of his country

Article 22
Everyone, as a member of society, has the right to social security.

Article 23
Everyone has the right to work.

Article 24
Everyone has the right to rest and leisure.

continued

Article 25
Everyone has the right to a standard of living adequate for health and well-being.

Article 26
Everyone has the right to education.

Article 27
Everyone has the right freely to participate in the cultural life of the community.

Article 28
Everyone is entitled to a social and international order in which the rights and freedoms set forth in this Declaration can be fully realized.

Article 29
Everyone has duties to the community in which alone the free and full development of his personality is possible.

Article 30
Nothing in this Declaration may be interpreted as implying for any State, group or person any right to engage in any activity or to perform any act aimed at the destruction of any of the rights and freedoms set forth herein.

See www.un.org and follow link for the Universal Declaration, available in 300 languages. See also related links at www.unhchr.org and to human rights education in particular where a range of teaching and learning resources is available, including a child-friendly version. See also Amnesty International site at www.ai.org.uk

The development of modern notions of universal human rights is an integral feature of the development of the UN itself. It is difficult in modern times to separate the development of universal human rights and the development of the United Nations. (Further guidance on research of the UN system can be found through the Dag Hammarskjöld Library, www.un.org/Depts/dhl/resguide)

On the level of regional-governmental or national-governmental alliances, from European Community to Commonwealth, these present a wealth of potential resources for religious educators, especially in the governance of multi-faith and plural democracies, and a sample of links is presented in Box 2.3. The Commonwealth is of particular interest for its historical links to the British Empire but also as an organisation that links countries of northern and southern hemispheres, illustrating a cultural and religious diversity that is reflected in everyday life in modern Britain.

In terms of the support networks for human rights, regional-governmental structures are essential for the maintenance of stated international orders. Where regional-governmental structures are relatively weak, as in the Organisation of African States (OAS), genocide on an unprecedented scale has been shown to be a reality unbelievable for the last decade of the twentieth century. Yet, Europe, with the oldest and arguably the strongest Convention on Human Rights – the 1950 European Convention on Human Rights appeared two years after the UN's Universal Declaration – saw 'ethnic cleansing'

Box 2.3
Parliament, government and the courts

10 Downing Street	www.pm.gov.uk
British Monarchy	www.royal.gov.uk
CommonLink	www.montageplus.co.uk/commonlink
Explore Parliament	www.explore.parliament.uk
Home Office	www.homeoffice.gov.uk
Locata MP	www.locata.co.uk/commons
UK Online	www.ukonline.gov.uk
Y Vote	www.learn.co.uk/yvote
YouGov.com	www.yougov.com
Young People's Parliament	www.ypp.org.uk
YourTurn.net	www.yourturn.net

UK relations within Europe, the Commonwealth and the United Nations

Council of Europe – Education	www.coe.fr/edu/eng
Erasmus Student Network	www.esn.org
European Schoolnet	www.eun.org
European Union	www.europa.org
European Union	www.europa.eu.int
Imperial War Museum	www.iwm.org.uk
Commonwealth Secretariat	www.thecommonwealth.org
United Nations	www.un.org

---

only two to three years before the barbarity of Rwanda. Modern warfare flagrantly flaunts all decrees on humanitarian treatment of prisoners and the weak and vulnerable (and frequently targets these).

The 1993 World Conference on Human Rights at Vienna thus reaffirmed 'the important and constructive role played by national institutions for the promotion and protection of human rights, in particular in their advisory capacity to the competent authorities, their role in remedying human rights violations, in the dissemination of human rights information, and education in human rights'. It also encouraged 'the establishment and strengthening of national institutions, having regard to the 'principles relating to the status of national institutions', recognising the right of each State to choose the framework which is best suited to 'its particular needs at the national level' (UN 1993: para. 36). Another aspect of regional-governmental implementation relates to those organs of a particular UN body that oversee arrangements for UN policy at a transnational and usually continental level. Again the importance of these arrangements was recognised at Vienna:

> Regional arrangements play a fundamental role in promoting and protecting human rights. They should reinforce universal human rights standards, as contained in

international human rights instruments, and their protection. The World Conference on Human Rights endorses efforts under way to strengthen these arrangements and to increase their effectiveness, while at the same time stressing the importance of cooperation with the United Nations human rights activities. The World Conference on Human Rights reiterates the need to consider the possibility of establishing regional and sub-regional arrangements for the promotion and protection of human rights where they do not already exist.

(UN 1993: para. 37)

Examples of regional-governmental human rights organisations are represented in Box 2.4.

Box 2.4

Human rights: regional-governmental organisations

Africa
Economic Commission for Africa (ECA) – Addis Ababa, Ethiopia
www.uneca.org
Organization of African Unity (OAU)
www.oau-oua.org

Americas and the Caribbean
Economic Commission for Latin America and the Caribbean (ECLAC) – Santiago, Chile
www.eclac.org
Organization of American States (OAS)
www.oas.org
(And related links to:
Inter-American Court of Human Rights
Inter-American Commission on Human Rights – IACHR
Inter-American Institute of Human Rights – IAIHR)

Asia
Economic and Social Commission for Asia and the Pacific (ESCAP) – Bangkok, Thailand
www.unescap.org
Economic and Social Commission for Western Asia (ESCWA) – Beirut, Lebanon
www.escwa.org.lb

Europe
Economic Commission for Europe (ECE) – Geneva, Switzerland
www.unece.org
Council of Europe Directorate General of Human Rights
European Commission against Racism and Intolerance (ECRI)
www.ecri.coe.int

continued

European Court of Human Rights
www.echr.coe.int
OSCE High Commissioner on National Minorities
www.humanrights.coe.int/minorities/index
OSCE Office for Democratic Institutions and Human Rights (ODIHR)
www.osce.org/odihr/cprsi/index

Beyond human rights as the basis of international law, wider aspects of citizenship impinge on religious educators. But for religious educators, human rights, the wrongs that these are designed to correct and prevent, and the responsibilities that are increasingly seen as part of human rights discourse through notions of global ethics (Kung and Schmidt 1998) provide a conceptual thread through the local, national and international political dimensions of citizenship. Many of these political dimensions – structural, organisational and conceptual – will be returned to when considering specific issues in Chapters 4 to 11.

Yet without religious and secular non-governmental organisations (NGOs), the global move towards universal human rights underpinning international law would be largely ineffective. Humanitarian assistance in times of crisis and development in the medium and longer terms are two areas where NGOs make UN an actuality on the ground. From Cafod to Jewish Aid, from the Red Cross to the Red Crescent, secular and religious NGOs play a crucial role in the promotion of every aspect of human rights. Human rights present a shared moral agenda for both secular and religiously based NGOs. The rights framework unites work on the ground at every level from local action to international consultation. For example, many NGOs have representative status at the UN, which means their views are solicited and listened to as part of UN policy-making. (For a general statement of the relationship between the UN and the NGOs follow the links for www.unog.ch/ESS_Mission_services/ngo/liaison.htm)

At Vienna, the role of NGOs was reaffirmed as essential to 'the promotion of all human rights and in humanitarian activities at national, regional and international levels':

> The World Conference on Human Rights appreciates their contribution to increasing public awareness of human rights issues, to the conduct of education, training and research in this field, and to the promotion and protection of all human rights and fundamental freedoms. While recognizing that the primary responsibility for standard-setting lies with States, the conference also appreciates the contribution of non-governmental organizations to this process. In this respect, the World Conference on Human Rights emphasizes the importance of continued dialogue and cooperation between Governments and non-governmental organizations.
>
> (UN 1993: para. 38)

Box 2.5 provides a small but representative sample of networks that provide links to the international community of NGOs. For religious educators, the major question here is how the rights framework has the capacity to unite in practice a disparate range of cultures and continents on matters of practical, active citizenship, when theoretical, philosophical and theological belief and practice so often divide. This provides ample justification for religious educators to explore a 'rights and responsibilities' route into citizenship.

Box 2.5
NGOs across continents

Africa
African Centre for the Constructive Resolution of Disputes (ACCORD)
www.accord.org.za
African Institute for Human Rights and Development
www.africaninstitute.org
Afronet
afronet.org.za/afronet
Southern African Human Rights NGO Network (SAHRINGON)
www.afronet.org.za/sahringon

Americas and Asia-Pacific
Asian Human Rights Commission (AHRC)
www.ahrchk.net
Asia-Pacific Forum on National Human Rights Institutions
www.apf.hreoc.gov.au
Asia Pacific Centre for Human Rights and the Prevention of Ethnic Conflict
wwwlaw.murdoch.edu.au/apchr
Directory of Organizations for Conflict Prevention in Asia and the Pacific
www.conflict-prevention.org
Human Rights in Latin America – LANIC
South Asia Human Rights Documentation Centre (SAHRDC)
www.hri.ca/partners/sahrdc
Lanic.utexas.edu/la/region/hrights
www.hrla.net
Human Rights Resource Center
www.hrusa.org

Europe
University of Essex Centre for Human Rights
www.essex.ac.uk/chr
Centre for Research in Human Rights, University of Surrey Roehampton (CRHR)
www.roehampton.ac.uk/crhr
Consortium of Minority Resources (COMIR)
www.lgi.osi.hu/comir
European Centre for Minority Issues (ECMI)
www.ecmi.de

continued

European Platform for Conflict Prevention and Transformation
www.euconflict.org
European Roma Rights Center (ERRC)
www.errc.org
Federal Union of European Nationalities (FUEN)
www.fuen.org
International Helsinki Federation for Human Rights (IHF)
www.ihf-hr.org
Minority Electronic Resources (MINELRES)
www.riga.lv/minelres
Open Society Institute Budapest
www.osi.hu/colpi
Statewatch
www.statewatch.org

General link for the UN and the NGOs
www.unog.ch/ESS_Mission_services/ngo/liaison

The end of history?

Decades after the UN Charter was signed, Fukuyama's (1992) much discussed sound-bite about 'the end of history' made claims that this ideal of how a society should operate was now genuinely accepted universally – liberal capitalism had 'won' the Cold War and liberal democracy based on a value system of shared human rights was now the unchallenged model for all societies. Yet the decade that followed Fukuyama's vast claims proved problematic and challenging for any notion that human rights were a universally accepted social and political reality.

The horrors which followed in the 1990s – East Timor, Kosovo, Kuwait, Rwanda, Somalia, the former Yugoslavia – and indeed 11 September 2001, do seem to militate against Fukuyama's thesis. On the surface, Fukuyama's would seem an uncomfortable and even untenable position. Yet, as the history of human rights indicates, this benchmark arose not from any great moral certainty but because of the absence of such (Johnson and Symonides 1999; Morsinky 1999). In short, the post-Holocaust years had shaken the international community into constituting or legislating for an understanding of a common moral standard. Today, especially with world conflicts fragmented into regional and local ethnic violence, the pragmatic need for this common moral framework remains as necessary as ever, however challenged our notions of universal virtue (MacIntyre 1985, 1988) or principle (Fish 1999). Even a 'postmodern' thinker like Rorty (1989), arguing that there is no non-circular reason why not to be cruel, agrees that to be cruel is the worst thing that one human being can do to another. Indeed, philosophers of education recognise that extremes of cruelty and violence are the main source for calls for a more moral education from the general public (Haydon 1999), and the avoidance of conscious human cruelty remains a form of categorical imperative. Its violation, the occurrence of atrocity in war or peace, still has the power to shock, even if the worst excesses of cruelty and abuse sometimes induce a sense of powerlessness in the distant observer. There remains, then, in pragmatic terms at least, a nominal consensus that this crowded earth needs a form of basic and legal standard by which to organise its various and diverse communities.

The best-known aspects of human rights are those under the heading of the International Bill of Human Rights including the founding Universal Declaration of Human Rights, the International Covenant on Economic, Social and Cultural Rights, and the International Covenant on Civil and Political Rights (Langley 1999; Robertson 1997; Forsythe 2000; Ryan 2000), in terms of the historical development of human rights in modern times. Wellman (2000) suggests a 'generational' approach: a first generation of civil and political rights; a second generation of social, cultural and economic rights; and an emergent third generation of 'human solidarity' rights. But he argues too that the crises of the 1990s suggest the proliferation of rights is empty rhetoric rather than moral progress.

Other critics (Mills 1998) suggest that human rights can be contested as cultural imperialism from New York and Geneva or a form of new sovereignty imposed by the west. Not surprisingly, some non-western societies, especially those organised around 'fundamentalist' religious or ideological principles, agree with such a view. Yet Fukuyama's end of history argument still holds: human rights remain the international benchmark for behaviour in the world today, however contested, and even if the world too often falls short of its own ideals.

The historic landmark in UK law was the Human Rights Act (1998) which, from October 2000, brought into direct effect within UK law the 1950 European Convention on Human Rights (Leckie and Pickersgill 1999; for legislation affecting other continents see Forsythe 2000: 110–38). The Home Office rightly describes this as one of the most significant pieces of constitutional legislation enacted in the United Kingdom 'and a key part of the Government's programme to encourage a modern civic society where the rights and responsibilities of our citizens are clearly recognised and properly balanced'. It will, the Home Office suggests, have 'a vital role to play in building a new human rights culture for the UK', defining this culture as a:

> modern society enriched by different cultures and faiths, given unity by a shared understanding of what is fundamentally right and wrong ... where people understand that rights and duties are two sides of the same coin, recognise the duties citizens owe each other and the wider community, and are willing to fulfil them.
>
> (Home Office 2000: 1–2)

In these national and international contexts, education is regarded as a crucial context for the promotion of human rights. This was made explicit in some detail in the Vienna Declaration and Plan of Action at the 1993 World Conference. The crucial point here is that education is seen as central in the development of an international human rights culture. The UN General Assembly continues, then, to be convinced of the importance of human rights education as a comprehensive, lifelong process integral to the promotion of human rights, officially proclaiming 1995–2004 as the United Nations Decade for Human Rights Education. Religious education has particular potential to address and promote all 'generations' of human rights: civil and political; social, cultural and economic; and those related to human solidarity. Aside from anything else, this inherent political potential presents opportunities for religious education to make a valid contribution to citizenship education. In order to achieve this potential, however, religious education needs to take more account of the political implications of teaching and learning in the representation of religious traditions. Evidence of an international perspective on such issues has been shown, led and inspired by Kung's work on a global ethic (Kung 1995; Kung and Schmidt 1998). Yet Kung's (1995) attempt to promulgate an authoritative platform for the 'Parliament' of the World's Religions, the closest we have really got to a full consideration of human rights in religious education, if well-intentioned, remains questionable. If human rights remain a basic value consensus, why the evident struggle – from an organisation far from democratic or truly repre-sentative – to define a global ethic when such is present within international law? However maligned the UN and its achievements are, religious traditions need to work with these notions of rights, and not re-invent new models of doubtful democratic status and with far less international credibility.

Yet, the absence of a significant political consciousness in religious education to address such issues is near self-evident. Beyond certain personal and social education-like issues, *pedagogies* of religious education in the past twenty to thirty years have clearly neglected structural and organisational aspects of political life as they impinge upon teaching and learning in religious education (again, Grimmitt 2000). Political philosophies are as far beyond the consideration of most notable religious educators as is any developed political theology for the study of religion in the classroom. To this extent at least, religious education has not kept pace with wider developments in the world of academic study of religion, where there appears to be a reversal in the once accepted trend of secularisation. Scholars like Casanova (1994) and J. and S.R. Haynes (1998, 2002) present undeniable evidence that religion has far from declined in prominence in public life. But we only need to watch television to realise that.

One natural way to counteract this neglect, theoretically and in terms of pedagogy, is by a heightened awareness and practical implementation of human rights education within the subject. For religious education, there is no area of political life more significant than universal human rights. The evidently inequitable distribution of human rights (especially in areas of health, education and basic living standards) and the obstacles to their universality, often from religious quarters, are major challenges for the religious educator and the teacher of citizenship.

Utopia/dystopia

The position from which we might begin to consider the issue of universal human rights from a religious perspective is an uncomfortable starting place. We need to balance religious education's often overly utopian agenda with the often dystopian global realities of cultural conflict – especially involving human rights, and particularly the part religions have played and continue to play in the abuse of these. Religious educators need to avoid, of course, a simplistic positive/negative thinking in relation to the present-day or historical political engagement of religious traditions – often so positive in the struggle for human rights and social justice. But assessment of religious traditions in relation to universal human rights may lead to political critiques. Religions do thus retain an occasional, if marked, political ambivalence in relation to recent and contemporary historical realities when it comes to universal rights.

However, from the approaches to pedagogy outlined in Grimmitt (2000), it is quite apparent that religious education has lacked, and continues to lack, both the astute historical depth and the sense of political reality that would easily allow such a consideration. One of the reasons for this is that the subject, understandably, does not wish to cause offence when, amongst other virtues, it proclaims tolerance, the need for understanding and the respect for diversity – all educational high-mindedness shared by citizenship. What we need to do is take more account of inherent power relations within and between religions, states and cultures; and to do so through a focus on religious education in relation to universal human rights, most widely understood.

Yet it is precisely such political issues that are seemingly beyond the unintentionally anodyne definitions of religion by official bodies like the Qualifications and Curriculum Authority (QCA) and their model syllabuses for religious education, useful as these might be in broader and more simplistic terms (QCA 1998a, 1998b). Uncritically written in complicity with the Faith Communities' Working Groups (QCA 1998c), how were religious educators to find any guidance on the critical (that is, often unpleasant) imperial histories and repressive present realities of religion if religious traditions themselves composed such guidance? It is understandable that educators no longer impose the agenda from entirely outside the traditions, and no one wishes to give overt offence. But there must be some means of critical engagement with traditions as living historical entities. In this regard, QCA's guidance on religious education and conflict – in the context of citizenship (see above, pp. 15–21) – is a tremendous advance.

If we are to have a critical consciousness in religious education it must be both historical and political. We cannot always try to seek unblemished religions or pure traditions. Indeed good phenomenology (Smart 1989) always tries to place religious culture in social and political context. So often, though, in religious education, the seemingly dysfunctional, impure manifestations of a religion are ignored or proclaimed as simply aberrations, a false political representation, an impure form of this religion or that, a cultural construction; however, as the religion manifests itself, so this is inevitably at least a part of what the tradition is as a whole. We may extend this analysis by suggesting that while religion does have a positive political role in the promotion of human rights and indeed suffers because of this involvement – religions continue to suffer immense persecution, for instance (Marshall 2000) – religious traditions have also actually been a culpable force in the international *denial* of human rights, especially in the repression of women and indigenous peoples, a process particularly notable in the history of imperialism (Harlow and Carter 1999; Hastings 1999).

Ayton-Shenker's brief but important UN Report, *The Challenge of Human Rights and Cultural Diversity*, sums up the contemporary potential for conflict:

> The end of super-power rivalry, and the growing North–South disparity in wealth and access to resources, coincide with an alarming increase in violence, poverty and unemployment, homelessness, displaced persons and the erosion of environmental stability. . . . At the same time previously isolated peoples are being brought together by the increasing integration of markets, the emergence of new regional political alliances, and remarkable advances in telecommunications, biotechnology and transportation that have prompted demographic shift.
>
> The resulting confluence of peoples and cultures is in an increasingly global, multicultural world brimming with tension, confusion and conflict in the process of readjustment to pluralism. There is an understandable urge to return to old conventions, traditional cultures, fundamental values, and the familiar, seemingly secure, sense of one's identity. Without a secure sense of identity amidst the turmoil of transition, people may resort to isolationism, ethnocentrism and intolerance.
>
> (Ayton-Shenker 1995: 1)

Ayton-Shenker argues that cultural relativism (the word fundamentalism is not used) is a potential threat to universal human rights, that the rights of an individual state or tradition cannot override rights established by majority international consensus. Indirectly highlighting charges against the UN itself, she argues convincingly that this hard-won consensus is a legal safeguard, 'not the cultural imperialism of any particular region or set of traditions':

> Most directly, human rights facilitate respect for and protection of cultural diversity and integrity, through the establishment of cultural rights embodied in instruments of human rights law. These include: the International Bill of Human Rights; the Convention on the Rights of the Child; the International Convention on the Elimination of all Forms of Racial Discrimination; the Declaration on Race and Racial Prejudice; the Declaration on the Elimination of all Forms of Intolerance and of Discrimination based on Religion or Belief; the Declaration on the Principles of International Cultural Cooperation; the Declaration on the Rights of Persons Belonging to National or Ethnic, Religious or Linguistic Minorities; the Declaration on the Right to Development; the International Convention on the Protection of the Rights of All Migrant Workers and Members of Their Families; and the ILO Convention No. 169 on the Rights of Indigenous and Tribal Peoples.
>
> (Ayton-Shenker 1995: 2)

Arguably, it is precisely because religions themselves are some of the worst offenders – historically through imperialism and today through fundamentalism – that religious educators need to take seriously dystopian global realities of which religions, often through ethnic and cultural identity, are a root cause (Gustafson and Juviler 1999). It is here that one might contend that it is only through a consciousness of politics and history that religious education can be truly engaged with citizenship.

The specific place of religion and human rights is not surprisingly then an emergent focus for academic analysis (Gearon 2002). Here a key theological reflection, written from within a South African context but of much wider applicability, is Villa-Vincencio's (1999) *A Theology of Reconstruction: Nation-Building and Human Rights*. Villa-Vincencio elucidates his review of harmful theological histories with a frighteningly abundant number of pertinent examples:

> The history of Christian crusaders in the 'old' world, conquistadors in the 'new' and the sense of manifest destiny among North American settlers are different manifestations of a similar theologised mission of conquest. Each is closely related to a theology of empire or nationbuilding. In more recent times, the missionary arm of British imperialism came close to totally destroying the cultural and religious identity of millions of colonised people. Theological support for Hitler's Third Reich contributed to the annihilation of six million Jews. And, most recently, theological support for Afrikaner nationalism has resulted in a cauldron of chauvinistic white supremacy and black resistance that has ultimately brought the richest and most technologically advanced country in Africa to its knees. Whatever the complexity of events which may or may not have contributed to this particular venture – a heretical, doctrinaire theology of apartheid has been the outcome.
>
> (Villa-Vincencio 1999: 19)

It is precisely these sorts of realities with which religious education in the UK at least has never really come to terms, and this may be because of the difficulty here of Britain facing its own imperial past when it wishes rightly to promote tolerance and understanding in an integrated multicultural present.

The precisely elaborated and reasoned curriculum agenda has yet to follow, and it may do so in the UK with the introduction of citizenship as a National Curriculum subject. Yet religious education has much to do to catch up. Even in QCA (2000a, 2000b) programmes of study we might ask whether this crucial political dimension is presented uncritically, even glibly, when under the heading of links between 'PSHE and Citizenship' we have, 'Issues in RE also clearly connect with social and political awareness (for example, human rights)' (QCA 2000b). Indeed, there are few substantive illustrations of where human rights might fit easily into the suggested programmes of study, even under the heading of modules such as 'Justice' – the Sikh scheme at key stage 3 having one of the few explicit references to the 1948 Universal Declaration (QCA 2000b). Citizenship provides these opportunities which are lacking in religious education at present.

Conclusion

These questions raise the case for an enhanced political awareness for religious education, and present human rights as but *one* important aspect of historical and contemporary international relations that would suit, arguably best of all, the citizenship agenda. Religious education will only be able to fulfil a developed role in the twenty-first century – including a strong relationship with developing areas like citizenship – if it continually reminds itself of the political dimensions of religion and the necessity for religious education to contribute actively to a raising of political as well as religious consciousness. The best models for emulation for such a political religious education are those that look at the place of religion in the context of an international values consensus that, however short of perfection, has been agreed by democratic process.

If one of the unstated flaws of religious education is its overly ambitious aims – which have included the transformation of spiritual, moral, social and cultural consciousness (Copley 1997, 2000) – then where such laudable aims fail is in idealistically neglecting harsh global, political, and so often dystopian, realities. As religious educators, we need here to take a hard look at religious traditions in order to examine honestly the clashes between their ideals and those reached by international democratic consensus.

As an important educational theme, human rights have the scope to bring real and enduring relevance to religious education. Just as religions themselves have always had prophetic traditions that have offered a voice for the voiceless, arguably, then, an understanding of the involvement of these same traditions in dystopian political realities encourages not only a greater sense of ambivalence but also urgency and relevance to religious education's fine utopian ideals. In practical terms Box 2.6 provides a starting point for further reflections.

Box 2.6
Human rights and religious education: question, discuss, research

Question and discuss

1   Why do you think religious education has so far neglected a political dimension? To what extent is this fair or unfair as an assumption?

2   Do religious traditions operate as democracies? Does it matter if they do not operate by the standards of state organisations?

3   Review the thirty articles of the Universal Declaration of Human Rights. Do any of these articles clash with fundamental beliefs in any of the world's major religious traditions – Buddhism, Christianity, Hinduism, Islam, Judaism or Sikhism?

4   The historical legacy of religious traditions has not always been a good one when one looks at the causes of wars, civil disputes and persecution done 'with God on our side', and, indeed, today, terrorist acts are undertaken in the name of religion. Is the

continued

argument that such justification of violence is 'not the true religion' sufficient as an argument to distance such violence from the tradition?

Research

5   Explore the possibilities for visits to and even work placements in leading international NGOs, local charities and religious communities.
6   Using the internet resources listed in Boxes 2.3, 2.4 and 2.5 explore what educational materials these groups have devised for citizenship, and especially citizenship and religious education.

This is not simply a matter of educational expediency – how can religious education contribute to citizenship? – but a real opportunity to develop and progress religious education into a vibrant new level of economic, social, political engagement. The case studies presented in Chapters 4 to 11 are an attempt to take important issues – from genocide to indigenous rights – and place them into a religious education context. Rights do not imply responsibility in and of themselves. Universal rights, as for example defined by the UN's 1948 Universal Declaration, are not dependent upon a government's or a state's beneficence. They are 'givens' of international relations, some more enforced and defended, admittedly, than others. Yet the focus on 'rights' – contested as all attempted universals are – will also incorporate the implied 'wrongs' of their contra-vention and notions of responsibility which are the less often stressed and more vulnerable dimension of rights discourse.

The rights approach will, as we shall see, interconnect with many aspects of citizenship, not all with the same force. Yet there is no claim here that a rights, wrongs and responsibilities approach will enable religious educators to fulfil all requirements of the National Curriculum Order for citizenship. If anything, religious education has generally set its sights unrealistically high. Neither religious education nor citizenship is a solution to all society's ills. Crick's much-cited and undemocratic profession that 'We aim at no less than a change in the political culture of this country both nationally and locally' is a naivety not shared by classroom teachers and educators. Nevertheless, from a potentially antagonistic meeting of religious education and citizenship we have the scope not only to teach citizenship through religious education but, ultimately, to have a religious education that transforms citizenship, and indeed religious education itself.

Chapter 3

Planning for citizenship through religious education

Introduction

Chapters 4 to 11 provide a range of themes and approaches to teaching citizenship through religious education using a rights and responsibilities approach. This chapter takes a close look at some structures that will be useful in a practical way for day-to-day and week-to-week planning. Given the suggested rights and responsibilities approach, however, it is certainly worth the teacher of religious education bearing in mind that such an approach should also inform the thinking behind as well as the practicalities of planning. In this regard, in citizenship perhaps more explicitly than other subjects, the rights of children themselves should be of paramount importance. Many of the UN's international standards regarding children are a reminder that the daily living conditions of children around the world are harsh. Practically all human rights standards apply or have special clauses pertaining to children but some of the child-specific pieces of official policy are presented in Box 3.1.

Box 3.1

International legal standards: defending children's rights

Declaration on the Rights of the Child (20 November 1959)
Declaration on Social and Legal Principles relating to the Protection and Welfare of Children, with Special Reference to Foster Placement and Adoption Nationally and Internationally (3 December 1986)
Convention on the Rights of the Child (20 November 1989, into effect 2 September 1990)
United Nations Rules for the Protection of Juveniles Deprived of the Liberty (14 December 1990)
United Nations Guidelines for the Prevention of Juvenile Delinquency (The Riyadh Guidelines) (14 December 1990)
Optional protocol to the Convention on the Rights of the Child on the involvement of children in armed conflict (25 May 2000, into effect 12 February 2002)

continued

Optional protocol to the Convention on the Rights of the Child on the sale of children, child prostitution and child pornography (25 May 2000, into effect 18 January 2002)

For full texts of these documents, follow links at www.un.hchr.org
Also useful are links to Children in Armed Conflict and Displacement: The Convention, Treaties and International Agreements (CRIN webpage).

Amongst these, and all other pieces of UN 'legislation', it is the 1989 Convention on the Rights of the Child that remains the single most ratified of all such UN conventions. While not all of the articles are of direct relevance to teachers, it is perhaps surprising how many resonate with educational policy in religious and citizenship education. Worth highlighting here are Articles 27 (reference to the child's 'physical, mental, spiritual, moral and social development), 29 (reference to the child's 'cultural identity, language and values, for the national values of the country in which the child is living') and 30 (reference to 'religious or linguistic minorities'). This is an instrument of immense importance about which too little has been made by educationalists in the United Kingdom, and which can be an inspiration in planning, and for this reason its principal articles are summarised as fully as possible in Box 3.2.

Box 3.2

Convention on the Rights of the Child
20 November 1989, entry into force 2 September 1990

Article 1 defines a child as 'every human being below the age of eighteen years unless under the law applicable to the child, majority is attained earlier'.
Article 2 presents States' responsibilities to 'respect and ensure the rights set forth in the present Convention to each child within their jurisdiction without discrimination of any kind, irrespective of the child's or his or her parent's or legal guardian's race, colour, sex, language, religion, political or other opinion, national, ethnic or social origin, property, disability, birth or other status'.
Article 3 states that 'In all actions concerning children, whether undertaken by public or private social welfare institutions, courts of law, administrative authorities or legislative bodies, the best interests of the child shall be a primary consideration.'
Article 4 presents States' responsibilities to 'undertake all appropriate legislative, administrative, and other measures for the implementation of the rights recognized in the present Convention. With regard to economic, social and cultural rights, States Parties shall undertake such measures to the maximum extent of their available resources and, where needed, within the framework of international co-operation.'
Article 5 presents the responsibilities of States to 'respect the responsibilities, rights and duties of parents or, where applicable, the members of the extended family or community

continued

as provided for by local custom, legal guardians or other persons legally responsible for the child, to provide, in a manner consistent with the evolving capacities of the child'.

Article 6 states that 'Every child has the inherent right to life.' It presents the responsibilities of States to ensure to 'the maximum extent possible the survival and development of the child'.

Article 13 states that 'The child shall have the right to freedom of expression; this right shall include freedom to seek, receive and impart information and ideas of all kinds, regardless of frontiers, either orally, in writing or in print, in the form of art, or through any other media of the child's choice.'

Article 14 states the rights of the child 'to freedom of thought, conscience and religion'.

Article 15 states the rights of the child 'to freedom of association and to freedom of peaceful assembly'.

Article 16 states that 'No child shall be subjected to arbitrary or unlawful interference with his or her privacy, family, home or correspondence, nor to unlawful attacks on his or her honour and reputation.'

Article 17 presents the responsibilities of States to 'recognize the important function performed by the mass media and shall ensure that the child has access to information and material from a diversity of national and international sources, especially those aimed at the promotion of his or her social, spiritual and moral well-being and physical and mental health'.

Article 27 presents the responsibilities of States to 'recognize the right of every child to a standard of living adequate for the child's physical, mental, spiritual, moral and social development'. The article also recognizes that 'the parent(s) or others responsible for the child have the primary responsibility to secure, within their abilities and financial capacities, the conditions of living necessary for the child's development'.

Article 28 presents the responsibilities of States to 'recognize the right of the child to education, and with a view to achieving this right progressively and on the basis of equal opportunity'. In particular, this involves making 'primary education compulsory and available free to all', the encouragement of secondary education and making higher education 'accessible to all on the basis of capacity by every appropriate means'.

Article 29 outlines some general comments on the implementation of Article 28. Here States have responsibilities to ensure General comment on its implementation, including:
'The development of the child's personality, talents and mental and physical abilities to their fullest potential;

The development of respect for human rights and fundamental freedoms, and for the principles enshrined in the Charter of the United Nations;

The development of respect for the child's parents, his or her own cultural identity, language and values, for the national values of the country in which the child is living, the country from which he or she may originate, and for civilizations different from his or her own.'

Article 30 states, 'In those States in which ethnic, religious or linguistic minorities or persons of indigenous origin exist, a child belonging to such a minority or who is indigenous shall not be denied the right, in community with other members of his or her group, to enjoy his or her own culture, to profess and practise his or her own religion, or to use his or her own language.'

Article 31 presents the responsibilities of States to 'recognize the right of the child to rest and leisure, to engage in play and recreational activities appropriate to the age of the child

continued

and to participate freely in cultural life and the arts'. It also suggests that States 'shall respect and promote the right of the child to participate fully in cultural and artistic life and shall encourage the provision of appropriate and equal opportunities for cultural, artistic, recreational and leisure activity'.

Article 32 presents the responsibilities of States to 'recognize the right of the child to be protected from economic exploitation and from performing any work that is likely to be hazardous or to interfere with the child's education, or to be harmful to the child's health or physical, mental, spiritual, moral or social development'.

For a full text of this document, follow links at www.unhchr.org

For a more child-centred focus, the UN and its agencies present a wealth of opportunities for developing this for teachers of religious education and citizenship, some of which are presented in Box 3.3.

Box 3.3
Children's rights links

Children's Rights
www.unicef.org/crc/index

The State of the World's Children 2000
www.unicef.org/sowc00/uwar2

World Education Forum: Dakar 2000
www.unicef.org/efa/results

The Progress of Nations 2000 – LOST CHILDREN
www.unicef.org/pon00/re

United Nations Educational, Scientific and Cultural Organization (UNESCO) – Paris, France
www.unesco.org

Planning for citizenship through religious education

There is much guidance that provides the essential – statutory and non-statutory – context for teaching and learning in citizenship as well as religious education. This chapter suggests a few generic approaches to teaching citizenship through religious education. The chapter is divided under a number of subheadings, as follows:

Preparation
Planning
Participation
Evaluation
Assessment

Preparation

Having a grasp of the official documentation is an essential start for any planning. Boxes 3.4 and 3.5 provide checklists for both citizenship and religious education.

Box 3.4

Key citizenship guidance: an online checklist

DEPARTMENT FOR EDUCATION AND SKILLS (www.dfes.gov.uk)
Health and Safety of Pupils on Educational Visits (HASPEV) (London: DfES)
The National Curriculum Handbook (London: DfES)
The Report of the Post-16 Citizenship Advisory Group (London: DfES)
OFFICE FOR STANDARDS IN EDUCATION (OFSTED) (www.ofsted.gov.uk)
Ofsted Handbook for the Inspection of Secondary Schools (London: HMSO)
QUALIFICATIONS AND CURRICULUM AUTHORITY (www.qca.org.uk)
Citizenship at Key Stages 3 and 4: Initial Guidance
Citizenship: A Scheme of Work for Key Stage 3: Teachers Guide
Citizenship: A Scheme of Work for Key Stage 4: Teachers Guide
Citizenship: A Scheme of Work for Key Stage 3
Citizenship: A Scheme of Work for Key Stage 4
Getting Involved: Extending Opportunities for Pupil Participation (KS3)
Staying Involved: Extending Opportunities for Pupil Participation (KS4)
Citizenship: A Guide for Senior Managers and Governors
TEACHER TRAINING AGENCY (www.canteach.gov.uk)
TTA/DfES (2002) *Qualifying to Teach* (London: TTA/DfES)
REPORTS (Available at www.citfou.org.uk)
B. Crick, (1998) *Education for Citizenship and the Teaching of Democracy in Schools: Final Report of the Advisory Group on Citizenship* (London: QCA) (The Crick Report)
Further Education Funding Council (1999) *Citizenship in Further Education* (London: DfEE/FEFC)

Box 3.5

Key religious education guidance: an online checklist

DEPARTMENT FOR EDUCATION AND SKILLS (www.dfes.gov.uk)
OFFICE FOR STANDARDS IN EDUCATION (OFSTED) (www.ofsted.gov.uk)
Ofsted Handbook for the Inspection of Secondary Schools (London: HMSO)
QUALIFICATIONS AND CURRICULUM AUTHORITY (www.qca.org.uk)
GCSE Short Course in Citizenship Studies and relevant GCSE Religious Studies courses can be found at the following examination board websites:
AQA: www.aqa.org.uk
EDEXCEL FOUNDATION: www.edexcel.org.uk
OCR: www.ocr.org.uk

Planning

Your school experience will involve you in planning teaching and learning activities for the short and medium term. Religious education and citizenship specific learning outcomes – attainment targets 1 and 2 in religious education – are dealt with through exemplars in Chapters 5 to 12. In addition, though, your teaching should make a contribution to key skills of:

- Communication – researching, discussion, information selection and sharing ideas
- Application of number – basic statistical analysis
- ICT – websites, databases
- Working with others – sharing, discussing, participation
- Improving own learning and performance – self-evaluation and target setting
- Problem solving – issues-based school and community participation

The pro forma in Box 3.6 provides guidance for short-term planning in religious education and citizenship activity – within and beyond the classroom. A pro-forma exemplar for medium-term planning is presented in Box 3.7.

Box 3.6
SHORT-TERM PLANNING

LESSON PLAN: Citizenship through religious education

Key stage: **Theme:**   **Link to programme of study:**

Date: **Class:**

Religious education learning outcomes (attainment targets 1 and 2)

AT 1

AT 2

Citizenship learning outcomes (using appropriate assessment criteria in relation to):
1   Knowledge and understanding about becoming informed citizens
2   Developing skills of enquiry and communication
3   Developing skills of participation and responsible action

Key skills checklist
Communication
Application of number
ICT
Working with others
Improving own learning and performance
Problem solving

Citizenship through religious education lesson/activity introduction

Activity 1

Activity 2

Activity 3

Conclusion

Differentiation

SEN (confidential – liaison with SEN co-ordinator)

Assessment opportunities
Informal (written formative, peer/self-assessment, oral question and answer)

1

2

Formal (diagnostic, summative, coursework/examination preparation)

1

2

Appropriate assessment criteria: Yes/No
Recorded: Yes/No
Feedback to pupils: Yes/No
Reported externally (for example, parents): Yes/No

Resources   **Detail**

1   ICT

2   TV/video/camcorder/projector

3   Visitor/guest speaker

4   Visit

Other

5

6

Teaching methods checklist
 1   Art
 2   Discussion
 3   Drama
 4   Experiential
 5   Formal assessment
 6   Group work
 7   Pair work
 8   Question and answer
 9   Research
10   Test
11   Visit
12   Visitor
13   Written work

Other
14
15
16

Box 3.7

MEDIUM-TERM PLANNING

SCHEME OF WORK: Citizenship through religious education

Key stage: Theme: Link to programme of study:

Date: Class:

Religious education learning outcomes (attainment targets I and 2)

AT I

AT 2

Citizenship learning outcomes (using appropriate assessment criteria in relation to):
I   Knowledge and understanding about becoming informed citizens
2   Developing skills of enquiry and communication
3   Developing skills of participation and responsible action

Key skills checklist
Communication
Application of number
ICT
Working with others
Improving own learning and performance
Problem solving

Citizenship through religious education scheme of work
Lesson outlines and learning outcomes in brief

Lesson I

Lesson 2

Lesson 3

Lesson 4

Lesson 5

Differentiation

SEN (confidential – liaison with SEN co-ordinator)

Assessment opportunities
Informal (written formative, peer/self-assessment, oral question and answer)

1

2

Formal (diagnostic, summative, coursework/examination preparation)

1

2

Appropriate assessment criteria: Yes/No
Recorded: Yes/No
Feedback to pupils: Yes/No
Reported externally (for example, parents): Yes/No

Resources	Detail
Resources	**Detail**
1 ICT	
2 TV/video/camcorder/projector	
3 Visitor/guest speaker	
4 Visit	
Other	
5	
6	

Teaching methods checklist
1   Art
2   Discussion
3   Drama
4   Experiential
5   Formal assessment
6   Group work
7   Pair work
8   Question and answer
9   Research
10 Test
11 Visit
12 Visitor
13 Written work

Other
14
15
16

Participation

So, will our approach to teaching citizenship through religious education really allow for the participation of the child as well as guidance and direction from well-intentioned adults? Does the participation planned take account of difference as well as the striving for understanding and accommodation? Is participation inclusive or exclusive? And here one of the key tensions in relation to active participation in citizenship as education – as outlined in the QCA documents – is the nature of democratic participation in schools themselves. It is important continually to revisit the question of what role schools have in developing the skills of participatory democracy. Can an essentially undemocratic institution, with little potential for genuine power sharing, offer a context for young people to experience democracy in action? 'Teaching *about* democracy' (Crick 1998) is unlikely to be as effective as genuinely experiencing and working in a democratic environment.

One of the most interesting models of participation in recent years is the 'ladder of participation' developed by Roger Hart (1997). It has been criticised for appearing to suggest a hierarchy of participation, with the final rung being the 'level' which should be attained by all. Hart himself does not claim this. He sees 'the "ladder" as a metaphor ... [and] useful in helping people think about children's developing capacity to participate'.

The ladder has eight rungs, the bottom three – manipulation, decoration, tokenism – are not, in Hart's view, participation at all.

1	Manipulation	Children do or say what adults suggest they do, but have no real understanding of the issues, OR children are asked what they think, adults use some of their ideas but do not tell them what influence they have had on the final decision.
2	Decoration	Children take part in an event, e.g. by singing, dancing or wearing T-shirts with logos on, but they do not really understand the issues.
3	Tokenism	Children are asked to say what they think about an issue but have little or no choice about the way they express those views or the scope of the ideas they can express.

The remaining five develop increasing levels of participation:

4	Assigned but informed	Adults decide on the project and children volunteer for it. The children understand the project, and know who decided they should be involved and why. Adults respect their views.
5	Consulted and informed	The project is designed and run by adults but children are consulted. They have a full understanding of the process and their opinions are taken seriously.
6	Adult-initiated, shared decisions with children	Adults have the initial idea but children are involved in every step of the planning and implementation. Not only are their views considered, but they are also involved in taking the decisions.

| 7 | Child-initiated and directed | Children have the initial idea and decide how the project is to be carried out. Adults are available but do not take charge. |
| 8 | Child-initiated, shared decisions with adults | Children have the ideas, set up the project, and invite adults to join with them in making decisions. |

As Hart explains, in any given project, young people may be involved in different ways, i.e. be on different rungs, and indeed may participate in different degree from project to project. His key concern is the development of genuine participation, and by working on rungs 4 to 8 children have the possibility of developing skills and knowledge 'depending upon their ability and interest in the project' (1997: 40).

Hart locates his ladder firmly within the Convention on the Rights of the Child (CRC). '[The CRC] emphasises strongly a right to grow into meaningful roles in society as full, democratic participating citizens' (1997: 21). The Convention contains articles that guarantee children's rights to survival and proper development (the provision articles), articles which guarantee protection from abuse and exploitation (the protection articles), and also articles of participation (Articles 12, 14, 15, 17, 23, 29 and 31) which state that 'children should know about their rights and be able to voice them, but they are also visionary articles which recognise children as developing citizens' (1997: 11).

In religious education, active participation will often involve religious communities, and religious educators have a long tradition of this. Chapters 4 to 11 show how these can be used for investigative purposes concerning attitudes and values. On a more generic note, active participation through such community involvement raises issues of pupils' health and safety. This is particularly evident if active participation involves taking groups of pupils – however large or small – beyond school premises. For this reason the DfES has issued guidance on safety during school visits and on activities involving active, community involvement – LEAs having responsibility for release of school time to allow for training – through the *Health and Safety of Pupils on Educational Visits (HASPEV)* document first published in 1998. Box 3.8 presents an overview of the likely stages involved in planning a visit.

Box 3.8

Stages in planning a visit

Outline proposal to head teacher or governing body, or LEA, seeking approval in principle. Proposals might include:

Visit's objectives
Likely date, duration, venue

continued

Pupil group, staffing
Resources, estimate of costs
(Proposals for longer visits may need to be made well before the start of the relevant academic year.)

Planning

Contact venue. Is it suitable for the group?
What are the transport options?
Who would lead the group and who would help to supervise it?
Who would pay for the visit?
Risk assessment
Exploratory visit

Substantive proposal to head teacher, or governing body, or LEA

Details of dates, risk assessment, emergency procedures, transport, insurance, costs, group membership, staffing

Shorter visits

Obtain approval and parental consent for visits involving years 1–3, or for day visits
Inform parents as necessary of shorter routine visits
Brief pupils
Go on visit monitoring the risks at all times

Residential and abroad

Obtain approval to prepare the visit subject to satisfactory preparation
Obtain final approval from LEA or governors, and parental consent
Go on visit monitoring the risks at all times
Evaluate

Final preparation

Information to and from parents
Briefing evening (meet the supervisors)
Brief pupils
Deposits/full payments by parents

DfES (2002) provides a detailed, cross-referenced assessment of the detail of each of these stages.

Box 3.9 provides a more extensive planning pro forma for active participation.

An audit of whole school provision will reveal what links with community groups are already established and through what subjects. One of the reasons an audit is so essential is that it can reveal gaps and overlap in provision. It can also identify levels and forms of

Box 3.9
Planning participation in citizenship through religious education

Use the Community Partner website (www.dfes.gov.uk/communitypartners) to examine case studies of what schools have done in relation to active participation and the following pro forma to develop an audit of possibilities.

I   The diversity of national, regional, religious and ethnic identities in the United Kingdom and the need for mutual respect and understanding

Schools have:

Alternative citizenship through religious education links could include:

- Nature of pupil participation
- Pupil use of ICT
- Pupil visit
- Community-based action (including potential work experience)

Key resource:

2   The work of parliament, the government and the courts in making and shaping the law

Schools have:

Alternative citizenship through religious education links could include:

- Nature of pupil participation
- Pupil use of ICT
- Pupil visit
- Community-based action (including potential work experience)

Key resource:

continued

3   The importance of playing a part in democratic and electoral processes

Schools have:

Alternative citizenship through religious education links could include:

- Nature of pupil participation
- Pupil use of ICT
- Pupil visit
- Community-based action (including potential work experience)

Key resource:

4   How the economy functions, including the role of business and financial services

Schools have:

Alternative citizenship through religious education links could include:

- Nature of pupil participation
- Pupil use of ICT
- Pupil visit
- Community-based action (including potential work experience)

Key resource:

5   The opportunities for individuals to bring about social change locally, nationally, in Europe and internationally

Schools have:

Alternative citizenship through religious education links could include:

continued

- Nature of pupil participation
- Pupil use of ICT
- Pupil visit
- Community-based action (including potential work experience)

Key resource:

6   The importance of a free press, and the media's role in society, including the internet, in providing information and affecting opinion

Schools have:

Alternative citizenship through religious education links could include:

- Nature of pupil participation
- Pupil use of ICT
- Pupil visit
- Community-based action (including potential work experience)

Key resource:

7   The rights and responsibilities of consumers, employers and employees

Schools have:

Alternative citizenship through religious education links could include:

- Nature of pupil participation
- Pupil use of ICT
- Pupil visit
- Community-based action (including potential work experience)

Key resource:

continued

8   **The United Kingdom's relations in Europe, including the European Union, the relations with the Commonwealth and the United Nations**

Schools have:

Alternative citizenship through religious education links could include:
*   Pupil use of ICT
*   Pupil visit
*   Community-based action (including potential work experience)

Key resource:

9   **The wider issues and challenges of global interdependence and responsibility, including sustainable development and Local Agenda 21**

Schools have:

Alternative citizenship through religious education links could include:
*   Pupil use of ICT
*   Pupil visit
*   Community-based action (including potential work experience)

Key resource:

pupil participation. Osler – at the Centre for Citizenship Studies in Education – provides a five-stage model of participative and experiential learning:

*   Pupils become aware
*   Pupils become more informed
*   Pupils develop their understanding
*   Pupils develop their own views and opinions
*   Pupils take action

(Osler 2001: 12)

There is also the important evaluative phase. One of the ways to make assessment itself active and participatory is to engage pupils in the process.

Evaluation

Community Partners is an initiative developed in conjunction with the DfES in response to the launch of citizenship in the National Curriculum. The focus is threefold:

1   Directory of community organisations
    Extensive list of groups that can offer support to schools
2   Case studies and project ideas
    A thematic, key stage subject area guide to active citizenship
3   Guidelines for good practice
    Quick guide to the context of community involvement
    A checklist of success factors for community involvement

The Community Partners initiative developed in conjunction with the DfES contains a useful 'Checklist of success factors for community involvement' which provides a working framework for teacher and pupil evaluation for key stages 3 and 4. The downloadable document has six headings:

1   The importance of explicit support for community involvement
2   The success factors for good practice
3   A methodology for active learning in the community
4   A checklist for quality community involvement
5   A checklist for developing community partnerships
6   Celebration and accreditation of pupils' learning and achievements

(www.csv.org.uk)

This generic guidance, presented in adapted form in Box 3.10, is essential for the evaluation process in citizenship through religious education.

Box 3.10

**Checklist of success factors for community involvement
in citizenship through religious education**

1 The importance of explicit support for community involvement
For ascertaining the level of support for religious education and citizenship through active learning in the community through your school: is citizenship through religious education:
•   Part of the development plan/mission statement for the school?
•   Clearly understood by the head teacher and the senior management team?

continued

- Understood by governors and parents?
- Supported by students through a school council or its equivalent?
- Supported through a wider curriculum which enables students to play a full and democratic part in the life of the school (e.g. peer learning/mentoring, mediation programmes, arts/science projects, sports coaching)?
- Contributed to directly by members of the local community and community organisations?
- Linked to an active partnership with local government? Are there opportunities for students to develop political literacy through contributing to local democratic processes?

2 The success factors for good practice

Schools with experience of community involvement have identified the following factors as critical to their success in citizenship. Factors applicable to citizenship through religious education include:

- Explicit support for citizenship education through community involvement from local stakeholders
- A clear methodology for active learning in the community
- A framework for active learning based on sound curriculum planning
- A school ethos which promotes mutual respect and equality of opportunity and encourages active participation
- A range of opportunities for pupils to develop as citizens through community involvement in and beyond the school
- Clear and mutually beneficial agreements between schools and their community partners
- Pupils' participation in defining, developing, implementing and reviewing their citizenship programmes/activities
- Recognition and accreditation of pupils' learning and achievements through community involvement in and beyond the school
- Designated member(s) of staff with responsibility for co-ordinating, monitoring and reviewing learning through community involvement in and beyond the school
- Continuing professional development for staff that addresses the specific needs of citizenship education and community involvement
- Mentoring and review of citizenship education that takes place annually and includes governors, management, staff, pupils and representatives from the communities served by the school

3 A methodology for active learning in the community

Active learning in the community – or service learning as it is often called in other parts of the world – is an education method which links meaningful student community service with academic learning, personal growth and civic responsibility. It is the process that links citizenship with community involvement.

Active learning in the community:

continued

- offers concrete opportunities for young people to learn new skills, think critically, and test new roles in an environment that encourages risk-taking and rewards competence
- is incremental, with progress from one year to the next
- is appropriate for use with all students and all curricular areas
- is integral to the taught and the whole curriculum (and not a bolt-on activity)
- provides structured time for the students or participants to reflect on what they have learned from the experience
- is accredited and celebrated
- responds to a wide range of needs in the school and wider community

Typically projects involve peer learning, community service, work on the environment, intergenerational projects and initiatives to develop communities through the arts, sciences and sport.

4 A checklist for quality community involvement
The following checklist has been distilled from experience in the United States and the UK. Does your active learning in the community programme:
- honour the purpose of community in the National Curriculum?
- strengthen service and academic learning through integrating the work within the mainstream taught and whole curriculum?
- feature in your Development Plan and publicly?
- provide concrete opportunities for young people to increase their knowledge, learn new skills, think critically and test new roles in an environment that encourages risk-taking and rewards competence?
- involve students in planning the project?
- involve students in the preparation and reflection?
- offer students guidance from experienced adults?
- recognise and celebrate the students' achievements?
- offer a meaningful contribution to the community?
- develop purposeful partnerships with the community and others involved in the project?
- provide staff and tutors with the appropriate training and professional development to promote effective service learning activities?
- have a designated member of staff with responsibility for co-ordinating and developing citizenship education throughout the school?

5 A checklist for developing community partnerships
When developing community partnerships be clear about:
- What you are looking for from your community partner
  Purpose
  Duration
  Staff commitments – lead contacts
  Expected outcomes
  Management/finance/administration
  Child protection issues
  Emergency procedures

continued

- The benefits that the partnership will bring both to the partner and to the school
- The contribution you will each make to the project
- The management at both ends. Who is the lead contact person with the partner organisation/school?
- The role of other people – community volunteers/people from local organisations
- Monitoring, evaluation and reporting arrangements. These need to be set up from the start rather than brought in at the end
- The contribution that the project will make to the whole school/wider community as well as to those immediately involved. For example, an oral history project with senior citizens might end with a publication/exhibition/Powerpoint show/assembly, etc.

6 Celebration and accreditation of pupils' learning and achievements
It is important that pupils' achievements in this area are recognised and celebrated as well as assessed and accredited. Celebration can take many forms and usually takes advantage of the opportunity for pupils involved in a project to tell others of their work and achievements. Community partners are often invited to share in the celebrations which can take place off the school premises as well as in school. An oral history project with older people, for example, can lead to an exhibition in the local library as well as in the school. Music, drama and the arts offer ready opportunities for public celebration, whereas IT projects are often celebrated on the web. It is important to give successful projects a high profile in the school and community. This generates many opportunities for the pupils and students to promote themselves through the media or marketing exercises.

Monitoring, recording, assessment and accreditation are always based on evidence that is systematically collected, recorded and reviewed by the students themselves through portfolios (personal and class) and Records of Achievement/progress files.

For source and further information visit: www.communitypartner.org.uk

Box 3.11 provides a checklist evaluating pupil and professional performance lesson-to-lesson.

Box 3.11

LESSON EVALUATION
Citizenship

Key stage: **Theme:**   **Link to programme of study:**

Class: **Date:**

I   To what extent have I achieved my stated learning outcomes?
Include supporting evidence (for example, assessment of students' work, student evaluations)

continued

2 Achievements/areas for development in relation to the Standards for Qualified Teacher Status
Professional values and practice

Knowledge and understanding

Teaching
Planning, expectations and targets

Monitoring and assessment

Teaching and classroom management

3 Targets for next lesson

Assessment

QCA also puts a strong emphasis upon the need for assessment at all key stages to have a participatory role for pupils and students, suggesting that at key stage 3, assessment in citizenship should enable pupils to:

- review the progress they have made during the key stage in each strand of the citizenship programme of study;
- reflect on their experiences across the curriculum and in broader community activities, and
- demonstrate some of the skills, knowledge and understanding they have acquired.

(QCA 2001b)

While there are no statutory arrangements for assessment at key stage 4, QCA suggests that schools may wish to provide their own form of certification as a means of recognising achievement and that the particular means of doing this 'will be based on the school's judgement about pupils' needs and abilities'. This may well be effective if students are sufficiently involved and motivated in the process and have found the activities involved in key stage 4 citizenship rewarding. However, such certification is likely to be held in less esteem than that for subjects examined and accredited externally. School-based certification will not be as useful to employers either. If taking the external assessment route, schools are advised that they 'should ensure before using an external qualification that it has been approved by the Secretary of State' and consult the list published annually by the DfES.

When delivering citizenship through religious education teachers need to balance carefully the demands of *both* subjects. So, for example, a number of examination boards have already developed syllabuses for delivering statutory requirements through Short Course GCSEs in Citizenship Studies and/or Religious Education. In order to receive recognition a GCSE Short Course in Citizenship – which must be designated Citizenship Studies – must give candidates the opportunities to:

- develop and apply knowledge and understanding about becoming informed citizens through and alongside development of skills of enquiry, communication, partici- pation and responsible action
- explore local, national and international issues, problems and events of current interest
- critically evaluate their participation within school and/or community activities

These aims translate into three assessment objectives pertinent for all such courses in Citizenship Studies. Thus a specification must require candidates to:

- AO1   demonstrate their knowledge and understanding of events of current interest; roles, rights and responsibilities; communities and identities; democracy and government; and relate them appropriately to individual, local, national and global contexts;
- AO2   obtain, explain and interpret different kinds of information including from the media, in order to discuss, form and express an opinion formally, and in writing, and demonstrate their ability to analyse and present evidence on a variety of issues, problems and events;
- AO3   plan and evaluate the citizenship activities in which they have partici- pated and demonstrate an understanding of their own contribution to them as well as recognising the views, experiences and contributions of others.

As these requirements are liable to change year-to-year, for a full appreciation of GCSE possibilities in religious education and citizenship the best source is the examination boards themselves:

AQA: www.aqa.org.uk
EDEXCEL FOUNDATION: www.edexcel.org.uk
OCR: www.ocr.org.uk

Of course GCSE Religious Studies offers very specific requirements and careful consideration will be needed for matching the requirements at this level through consultation with the relevant examination board.

Conclusion

Citizenship as a National Curriculum subject is in its infancy. Collaboration with religious education remains at an early stage of development. Systematic planning will be needed to ensure that any initiatives are carefully planned, monitored, evaluated and assessed. Religious education has the potential to be threatened by citizenship (in terms of competition for curriculum space), and to enrich and be enriched by the many opportunities that the new National Curriculum subject offers. Box 3.12 provides an opportunity to reflect on these and related planning issues.

Box 3.12

Planning for citizenship through religious education: question, discuss, research

Question and discuss

1   Review the Convention on the Rights of the Child (Box 3.2). How could teaching citizenship through religious education contribute to the promotion of these rights?
2   In the same way as you reviewed the thirty articles of the Universal Declaration of Human Rights in the light of the world's religions, review the Convention on the Rights of the Child. Do any of these articles clash with fundamental beliefs in any of the world's major religious traditions – Buddhism, Christianity, Hinduism, Islam, Judaism or Sikhism?
3   Visit one or more of the links to children's rights presented in Box 3.3. Think of how you might use one of these sites for integration of ICT, RE and citizenship.
4   Review the exam board websites presented in Box 3.5. How might your suggestions for the last exercise (question 3 above) be used in a relevant GCSE-level course?
5   Now, using ideas from questions 1, 2, 3 and 4 above, use Boxes 3.6 and 3.7 from this chapter to develop a more formal example of short- and medium-term planning using the theme of children's rights through religious education.
6   Boxes 3.8 and 3.9 look at the practicalities necessary in planning a successful visit. Discuss ideas for a visit that might represent an ideal mix of citizenship and religious education at key stage 3 and/or 4.
7   If you have undertaken a recent visit as part of training or teaching, in the light of experiences here critically reflect on the success factors for community involvement in citizenship through religious education presented in Box 3.10.

continued

Research

8 Devise a small-scale, action research project reviewing children's experiences of citizenship through religious education.
9 If you are part of a teaching team within a school, undertake a similar small-scale research project evaluating the experiences of those involved in teaching citizenship through religious education.
10 For longer-term professional development, and for the more ambitious potential researcher, consult with a local university on undertaking more formal research in the area, perhaps as part of M.Phil./Ph.D. research.

Citizenship through religious education: rights, wrongs and responsibilities

Part II

Citizenship through
religious education: rights,
wrongs and responsibilities

Chapter 4

Genocide through religious education

Introduction

This chapter deals with genocide. I read this sentence again and find it inadequate. This chapter does not 'deal' with genocide any more than any other chapter or article or research study or book can 'deal' with genocide. Genocide is a vacuum into which all notions of human goodness, all thought of rights, all optimism, can sink without trace. What this chapter attempts to do is to provide some brief space for the religious educator to reflect – on the fact that genocide fundamentally challenges all notions of civilisation, culture, social order. A space to reflect on the fact that, of all species that have ever existed, only human beings do this to each other. Genocide is an amoral vacuum, a black hole into which all social and political order is sucked until the point of singularity, nothingness. Yet history has recorded its aftermath. As we look back from the twenty-first century, the trace of this history still blazes across the decades, every decade, of the twentieth. If there is any justification for religious education making a contribution to citizenship, it is to learn the lessons about human nature and human history that genocide teaches: its origins, the horror of its enactment, its punishment and its prevention.

Genocide: historical-legal-political background

At the World Conference on Human Rights at Vienna in 1993, condemnation of 'massive violations of human rights especially in the form of genocide, ethnic cleansing and systematic rape of women in war situations' (para. 28) was notable amongst the laments of the gathered international community. Such laments came a matter of months after full revelation of horror in the Balkans in the early 1990s, and only two years before the numerically even more atrocious figures of mass killings in Rwanda and neighbouring countries. And behind the statistics of genocide (see Box 4.1) are the personal stories of suffering of individuals and families, friends and relatives.

The late twentieth century witnessed massive failure by the international community to prevent repetition of the historical scars that marred the early and middle part of the century. Such dystopian historical realities are an indication of apparent political impotence by the United Nations. The history of such apparent failure goes back to the origins of the United Nations. The day before the UN General Assembly signed the

Universal Declaration in December, it approved, on 9 December, the 1948 Convention against Genocide, with its famous preamble:

> Having considered the declaration made by the General Assembly of the United Nations . . . that genocide is a crime under international law, contrary to the spirit and aims of the United Nations and condemned by the civilized world, recognizing that at all periods of history genocide has inflicted great losses on humanity, and being convinced that, in order to liberate mankind from such an odious scourge, international co-operation is required.

Its vision of utopia, epitomised by its Charter (see Box 2.1), too often has revealed a reality for some of nothing better than hell on earth.

In a world weary of two world wars and with a clear awareness of the systematic Nazi and related mass-killing, the Convention was born out of a 'never again' mentality. Since 1948, however, genocide, defined here as the systematic and deliberate targeting for extinction of particular sections of a population, has happened again and again, and yet again. Ryan's (2002) study of the United Nations includes some depressing figures on its regularity not only decade-to-decade but within each decade since the late 1940s, and this is clearly illustrated in Box 4.1.

Box 4.1

Statistics on deaths of particular population sections

Date	State	Victims	Deaths
1943–57	USSR	Chechens, Ingushi, Karachai	230,000
1944–68	USSR	Crimean Tartars, Meskhetians	57,000–175,000
1955–77	China	Tibetans	Not available
1959–75	Iraq	Kurds	Not available
1962–72	Paraguay	Ache Indians	90,000
1963–4	Rwanda	Tutsis	5,000–14,000
1963	Laos	Meo Tribesmen	18,000–20,000
1965–6	Indonesia	Chinese	0.5–1 million
1965–73	Burundi	Hutus	103,000–205,000
1966	Nigeria	Ibos in North	9,000–30,000
1966–84	Guatemala	Indians	30,000–63,000
1968–85	Philippines	Moros	10,000–100,000
	Equatorial Guinea	Bubi Tribe	1,000–50,000
1971	Pakistan	Bengalis of Eastern Pakistan	1.25–3 million
1971–9	Uganda	Karamajong, Acholi, Lango	100,000–500,000
1975–9	Cambodia	Muslim Cham	
1975–98	Indonesia	East Timorese	60,000–200,000
1978–	Burma	Muslims in border regions	Not available

continued

Date	State	Victims	Deaths
1979–86	Uganda	Karamanjong, Nilotic Tribes, Bagandans	50,000–100,000
1981	Iran	Kurds, Bahais	10,000–20,000
1983–7	Sri Lanka	Tamils	2,000–10,000
1992–5	Bosnia-Herzegovina	Mainly Bosnian Muslims	200,000
1994	Rwanda	Tutsis	0.5–1 million

(Ryan 2002)

Since the failures of the 1948 Genocide Convention (Box 4.2) and related international standards (see Box 5.3) to effectively curtail post-Holocaust instances of systematic and mass killing, the practice known as genocide and its punishment through international human rights law (Schabas 2000) have become the object of serious academic study. Analyses vary from generic (Ball 1999; Kressel 2001), comparative (Chorbajian and Shirnian 1999; Hinton 2002; Lorey and Beezley 2002) and even encyclopaedic (Charny 1999) treatments, to assessments of the regional and specific, from Armenia (Dadrian 1999) and Cambodia (Chandler 2001) to Bosnia-Herzegovina (Weine 1999) and Rwanda (Gourevitch 1999). The defining genocide of the Holocaust remains an abiding academic interest for historians in ever-new guises and nuances, such as a recent interpretation of the Nazi atrocities as an economic as well as ideological process (Allen 2002).

Box 4.2

Convention on the Prevention and Punishment of the Crime of Genocide
9 December 1948, entry into force 12 January 1951

This statement is the basis of the nineteen articles of the Convention.

Article 1 states that 'Genocide, whether committed in time of peace or in time of war, is a crime under international law' which the international community undertakes to prevent and to punish.

Article 2 states that 'In the present Convention, genocide means any of the following acts committed with intent to destroy, in whole or in part, a national, ethnical, racial or religious group, as such:
(a) Killing members of the group;
(b) Causing serious bodily or mental harm to members of the group;
(c) Deliberately inflicting on the group conditions of life calculated to bring about its physical destruction in whole or in part;
(d) Imposing measures intended to prevent births within the group;
(e) Forcibly transferring children of the group to another group.'

Article 3 states that the following acts shall be punishable:
'(a) Genocide;

continued

(b)   Conspiracy to commit genocide;
(c)   Direct and public incitement to commit genocide;
(d)   Attempt to commit genocide;
(e)   Complicity in genocide.'

Article 4 states that 'Persons committing genocide or any of the other acts enumerated in article III shall be punished, whether they are constitutionally responsible rulers, public officials or private individuals.'

Article 5 states that 'The Contracting Parties undertake to enact, in accordance with their respective Constitutions, the necessary legislation to give effect to the provisions of the present Convention, and, in particular, to provide effective penalties for persons guilty of genocide or any of the other acts enumerated [in Article 3].'

Article 6 states that 'Persons charged with genocide or any of the other acts enumerated in article III shall be tried by a competent tribunal of the State in the territory of which the act was committed, or by such international penal tribunal as may have jurisdiction with respect to those Contracting Parties which shall have accepted its jurisdiction.'

Article 7 states that 'Genocide and the other acts enumerated shall not be considered as political crimes for the purpose of extradition. The Contracting Parties pledge themselves in such cases to grant extradition in accordance with their laws and treaties in force.'

Article 8 states that 'Any Contracting Party may call upon the competent organs of the United Nations to take such action under the Charter of the United Nations as they consider appropriate for the prevention and suppression of acts of genocide or any of the other acts enumerated in article III.'

Articles 9 to 19 concern formalities between contracting parties (**Article 9**), the translation of the document (**Article 10**), signing and ratification (**Article 11**), extending applicability of the Convention to the foreign territories of the contracting parties (**Article 12**), means by which the Convention comes into force (**Article 13**), period of effectiveness of the Convention (**Article 14**), denunciation (**Article 15**), processes for revision (**Article 16**), procedures for notifying signatories to the Convention (**Article 17**), deposition of the original Convention in the UN archives (**Article 18**), registration of the Convention with the Secretary-General of the UN (**Article 19**).

For the full text, follow links at www.unhchr.org

Box 4.3

International legal standards: defending against genocide

War crimes and crimes against humanity, including genocide
Convention on the Prevention and Punishment of the Crime of Genocide (9 December 1948, into effect 12 January 1951)
Convention on the Non-Applicability of Statutory Limitations to War Crimes and Crimes against Humanity (29 November 1968, into effect 11 November 1970)
Principles of international co-operation in the detection, arrest, extradition and punishment of persons guilty of war crimes and crimes against humanity (3 December 1973)

continued

Humanitarian law

Geneva Convention for the Amelioration of the Condition of the Wounded and Sick in Armed Forces in the Field (21 April–12 August 1949, into effect 21 October 1950)

Geneva Convention for the Amelioration of the Condition of Wounded, Sick and Shipwrecked Members of Armed Forces at Sea (21 April–12 August 1949, into effect 21 October 1950)

Geneva Convention relative to the Treatment of Prisoners of War (21 April–12 August 1949, into effect 21 October 1950)

Geneva Convention relative to the Protection of Civilian Persons in Time of War (21 April–12 August 1949, into effect 21 October 1950)

Protocol Additional to the Geneva Conventions of 12 August 1949, and relating to the Protection of Victims of International Armed Conflicts (Protocol I) (8 June 1977, into effect 1979)

Protocol Additional to the Geneva Conventions of 12 August 1949, and relating to the Protection of Victims of Non-International Armed Conflicts (Protocol II) (8 June 1977, into effect 1979)

For the texts of all these documents, follow the links on www.unhchr.ch

---

With the prevalence of post-Holocaust occurrences of genocide and ethnic cleansing, there are studies that question its uniqueness (Rosenbaum 2001; Smith 2002; Waller 2002).

Aside from studies related to the role of nationalism and ethnicity (Ryan 2002; cf. Ryan 2000), the role of religion in genocide has received fairly scant attention, with some exceptions (Bartov and Mack 2001). In international relations this is being rectified. It is not simply a post-September 11 context that has changed this. The UN Research Institute for Social Development (UNRISD), based in Geneva, Switzerland (www.unrisd. org/), has for some time been developing a number of research programmes directed at religious, cultural and ethnic conflict. Religious educators will find the following helpful:

The Search for Identity Ethnicity Religion and Political Violence
www.unrisd.org/engindex/publ/list/op/op6/op06–03

Ethnic Violence Conflict Resolution and Cultural Pluralism
www.unrisd.org/engindex/publ/list/conf/eth1/eth1–04

Ethnic Diversity and Public Policy: An Overview
Www.unrisd.org/engindex/publ/list/op/op8/op08–05

One of the major developments in human rights is the development of the International Criminal Court (ICC) which presents opportunities for those guilty of war crimes and crimes against humanity to be brought to justice. For full details, including controversies surrounding US claims for exemption, see the ICC and related sites listed in Box 4.4.

Box 4.4
ICC links

UN International Criminal Court
http://www.un.org/law/icc/index
International Coalition for the ICC
http://www.igc.org/icc/html/coalition
Council of Europe page on the International Criminal Court
http://www.legal.coe.int/criminal/icc
Amnesty International ICC site
http://www.amnesty.org.uk/action/camp/icc/index.shtml
Women's Caucus for Gender Justice
http://www.iccwomen.org/icc/index
International Criminal Court Internet Library
http://www.lib.uchicago.edu/~llou/icc.html#internet
International Criminal Tribunal for Rwanda
http://www.un.org/ictr
International Criminal Tribunal for the Former Yugoslavia
http://www.un.org/icty

Genocide through religious education: planning notes

Beth Shalom, dedicated to the remembrance and prevention of, as well as education about, the Holocaust (and genocide more widely), provides a range of accessible teaching and learning resources, many of which are explicitly related to religious education, and as many providing for cross-curricular links. The Beth Shalom Web Centre contains three related sites:

> Holocaustcentre.net – the Beth Shalom Holocaust Centre
> Holocausthistory.net – an introduction to the Holocaust in historical context
> Holocaustbookstore.net – an online retail store run by Beth Shalom, specialising exclusively in Holocaust- and genocide-related books and resources

Box 4.5 lists other educational links to genocide with potential connections to themes within religious education.

Box 4.5
Genocide through religious education:
learning resource links

International Crisis Group
www.crisisweb.org

continued

FEWER
www.fewer.org

Genocide Watch
www.genocidewatch.org

International Alert
www.international-alert.org

The Organization for Security and Co-operation in Europe (OSCE)
www.osce.org

Prevent Genocide International
www.preventgenocide.org

Saferworld
www.saferworld.co.uk

Such developments are indicative of the growing importance of genocide as an aspect of compulsory education, are in line with official governmental interest in the UK (DfEE 2000) and relate integrally to the arrival of National Curriculum citizenship.

Given the foregoing historical-legal-political background, what we need to do as religious educators is integrate the key aspects of genocide appropriate to a religious education context. This means identifying the explicit religious context and planning for explicitly religious education learning outcomes. While presenting particular lesson plans might be prescriptive, what is offered here – adapting the structure of the QCA *Model Syllabuses for Religious Education* – is a suggested typology (Boxes 4.6.1 to 4.6.3), identifying:

* Attainment targets in religious education
* Skills and processes in religious education
* Attitudes in religious education

What follows (Box 4.6.4) is a series of suggested links for this theme to National Curriculum citizenship.

Box 4.6.1

Genocide: attainment targets in religious education

Attainment target 1: Learning about religions
Identify a critical period in the history of genocide and give an account of the cultural, ethnic and/or religious involvement and/or response to events – the Holocaust, Rwanda, the former Yugoslavia.

continued

Explore religious language, stories and symbolism that enable an individual or a people to come to terms with genocide.

Attainment target 2: Learning from religions
Give an informed and considered response to the religious and moral issues surrounding the individual and collective human suffering behind the statistical horrors of genocide.

Reflect on what might be learned – if anything can be learned – from genocide in the light of one's own beliefs and experience.

Identify and respond to questions of meaning with which genocide confronts humanity.

Box 4.6.2

Genocide: skills and processes in religious education

Investigation
Asking relevant questions about genocide: Why? Why again?
Knowing how to use different types of sources as a way of gathering information about genocide.
Knowing what may constitute evidence for understanding religions and their participation in or status as victims of genocide.

Interpretation
The ability to draw from artefacts, works of art, poetry and symbolism reflecting genocide and the ability to suggest the meaning of religious texts in the face of untold suffering.

Reflection
The ability to reflect on feelings, relationships, experience, ultimate questions, beliefs and practices in the face of the death camps, the torture chamber, the rape of the defenceless.

Empathy
The ability to consider the thoughts, feelings, experiences, attitudes, beliefs and values of others who suffer; and to reflect on the power of imagination in creating suffering on a massive scale; and to identify feelings such as love, wonder, forgiveness and sorrow that overcome the worst of horror.

Evaluation
The ability to debate issues of religious significance with reference to evidence and argument and how evidence and argument disarm and create incredulity at the power of human beings' inhumanity.

Analysis
Distinguishing between opinion, belief and fact, especially in assessments of propaganda,

continued

prejudice, and the extremes of discrimination, often targeted at cultural, ethnic and religious minorities.

Synthesis
Linking significant features of religion together in a coherent pattern – can we make sense of the carnage?

Application
Making the association between religions and individual, community, national and international life, identifying key religious values and their interplay with secular ones, especially in the role of NGOs.

Expression
The ability to explain the persistence of concepts, rituals and practices associated with religion, against all odds, in the face of history.
The ability to identify and articulate matters of deep conviction and concern, and respond to religious questions through a variety of media – art, music, the novel.

Box 4.6.3

Genocide: attitudes in religious education

Commitment
Understanding the importance of commitment to a set of values by which to live one's life, often against all reason for hope.

Fairness
Considering other views carefully; willingness to consider evidence and argument; the readiness to look beyond surface impressions to signs of hope, truth, remembrance and eventual reconciliation.

Respect
Recognising in the face of genocide the need to respect those who have different beliefs and customs; recognising the rights of others to hold their own views; the avoidance of ridicule; and the discernment of what is worthy of respect and what is not.

Self-understanding
Developing a mature sense of self-worth and value; developing the capacity to discern the personal relevance of religious questions, and relative good fortune.

Enquiry
Curiosity and a desire to seek the truth; critical reflection on existential and metaphysical questions about the nature of human beings posed by the horror of genocide.

Box 4.6.4

Genocide through religious education: National Curriculum citizenship links

Knowledge and understanding about becoming informed citizens
1   Pupils should be taught about:
a   the legal and human rights and responsibilities underpinning society and how they relate to citizens, including the role and operation of the criminal and civil justice systems
POSSIBLE RELIGIOUS EDUCATION LINKS: Explore the role of ethnicity, culture and religion in the Holocaust and genocide more generally, including legal protections by the international community through the UN.
b   the origins and implications of the diverse national, regional, religious and ethnic identities in the United Kingdom and the need for mutual respect and understanding
POSSIBLE RELIGIOUS EDUCATION LINKS: The response of religious communities in the United Kingdom to genocide – including survivors – through study and community links.
f   the opportunities for individuals and voluntary groups to bring about social change locally, nationally, in Europe and internationally
POSSIBLE RELIGIOUS EDUCATION LINKS: Use of NGOs, Holocaust resource centres and museums in Holocaust and genocide education.
g   the importance of a free press, and the media's role in society, including the internet, in providing information and affecting opinion
POSSIBLE RELIGIOUS EDUCATION LINKS: Propaganda by and against cultural, ethnic and religious groups as a means to support and justify genocide.
i   the United Kingdom's relations in Europe, including the European Union, and relations with the Commonwealth and the United Nations
POSSIBLE RELIGIOUS EDUCATION LINKS: The International Criminal Court, and the tribunal set up to investigate and punish crimes against humanity in the former Yugoslavia and Rwanda.

Developing skills of enquiry and communication
2   Pupils should be taught to:
a   research a topical political, spiritual, moral, social or cultural issue, problem or event by analysing information from different sources, including ICT-based sources, showing an awareness of the use and abuse of statistics
b   express, justify and defend orally and in writing a personal opinion about such issues, problems or events
c   contribute to group and exploratory class discussions, and take part in formal debates
POSSIBLE RELIGIOUS EDUCATION LINKS: See Question, discuss, research activities in Box 4.7.

Developing skills of participation and responsible action
3   Pupils should be taught to:

continued

> a   use their imagination to consider other people's experiences and be able to think about,
>   express, explain and critically evaluate views that are not their own
> b   negotiate, decide and take part responsibly in school- and community-based activities
> c   reflect on the process of participating
> POSSIBLE RELIGIOUS EDUCATION LINKS: See Question, discuss, research activities in
> Box 4.7.

In planning for citizenship through religious education, it is crucial that neither the explicit religious education nor conscious citizenship elements of delivery are lost.

Conclusion

At the opening of this chapter, it was suggested that, 'If there is any justification for religious education making a contribution to citizenship, it is to learn the lessons about human nature and human history that genocide teaches: its origins, the horror of its enactment, its punishment and its prevention.' It is possible to stand by such a statement. Yet, while essential, genocide is as difficult a subject to draw to a close as it is to open for discussion. Good teaching always prepares the learner for a yearning to know more or question further. Box 4.7 is an attempt to raise some of the questions opened up by this chapter on genocide through religious education.

Box 4.7

Genocide through religious education: question, discuss, research

Question and discuss

1   Where was God in Auschwitz, or Belsen, or the former Yugoslavia or Rwanda?
2   Can any ultimate good come out of genocide?
3   What does genocide do to change our understanding of citizenship?
4   Does genocide make notions such as citizenship, civilisation, society and culture a
     veneer?
5   Does genocide reveal human beings as they really are?
6   What would Jesus – or any other religious figure – say or do about genocide?
7   How does genocide challenge fundamental religious (or any form of) beliefs about
     meaning and purpose in life?

Research

8   Use one of the websites listed in Box 4.5. Find one instance of where religious persons

continued

---

or groups are specific or incidental *victims* of genocide. Find one instance of where religious persons or groups are specific or incidental *perpetrators* of genocide.

9   Visit the Beth Shalom website. Find one educational resource for use in teaching genocide in religious education.

10 With the history department in your school, explore possibilities for a joint visit to the Imperial War Museum (www.ipm.org), particularly the Holocaust exhibition. The Imperial War Museum also contains a vast range of materials for religious educators to use in relation to ethical issues and moral dilemmas raised by war more generally, including the 'Just War', development issues and conflict, and terrorism. The museum contains two significant galleries of art from the First and Second World Wars.

Chapter 5

Asylum through religious education

Introduction

The late twentieth and early twenty-first centuries have seen an international increase in numbers of those seeking refugee status (Audit Commission 2000; UNHCR 2000, 2001, 2002; UN 2002j, 2002l, 2002q). The media often couch discussions of asylum and refugee status in emotive terms. Words and expressions like 'swamped' and a 'flood of refugees' are designed to create at worst alarm and even panic, a sense of a situation out of control, and at the very least disquiet and unease amongst those with established status as citizens. Asylum seekers and refugees are at the margins of citizenship. They are often formally citizens, sometimes with few rights, of countries where it is no longer safe or viable for them to live. Few countries openly welcome such newcomers to their borders and local neighbourhoods are often openly hostile to such strangers in their midst. For the religious educator asylum and refugee status present unique opportunities. It is one area where school communities, especially but not exclusively in urban areas, will have direct experience. Yet just because asylum seekers are from diverse cultural, ethnic and religious backgrounds, it does not mean that the religious educator should have sole expertise. Still, the religious and cultural element does give the religious educator some degree of authority to address this contentious aspect of citizenship.

Asylum: historical-legal-political background

With a world population of over 6 billion and resources unequally distributed, the issue is a genuinely complex and problematic one, and not liable to easy solutions (Steiner 2000). There are many reasons why people seek to leave one country for another. Article 14 of the Universal Declaration of Human Rights states plainly that everyone has the right to seek and to enjoy in other countries asylum from persecution. Many flee from such realities (Refugee Council 1997). War, as always, is another factor prompting sudden shifts in migration (Mawson *et al.* 2000), with many of those seeking security being children. Increasingly the reasons for migration are economic (UNHCR 2001), and arise from a sense of economic desperation in situations of extreme humanitarian need (Robinson 2001; Helton 2002). If migrant workers present a different set of issues from refugees, similar human rights issues still surface for both, especially in terms of access to education, health care and social welfare (Hayfield 2001; Prince *et al.* 2002; Refugee Council/Oxfam 2002).

In the post-Cold War period, intra-border ethnic conflicts (as we saw in Ryan's figures on genocide in the last chapter) and struggles over national identity (M. Brown 2001) have been more predominant than inter-state tensions. (Afghanistan and Iraq are part-exceptions.) If Europe and the west are the regions to which refugees and asylum seekers naturally incline, it is a worthy reminder that the greatest numbers of refugees witnessed during the twentieth century originated from Europe itself: in the period prior to the rise of Hitler and the Third Reich in Nazi Germany, the period during the Second World War itself, and in the years directly after the Second World War (Conway and Gotovitch 2002). These refugees often bestowed on their receiving countries great scientific and cultural benefits (Medawar 2000), a pattern which is not uncommon, as the Refugee Council's study of the benefits brought by a range of asylum seekers over the decades shows. There are equally some refugee situations, notably that of the Palestinians, that are intractably linked to the end of the Second World War, the ending of the British Empire and the formation of new States like Israel – for which sections of the UN Relief and Works Agency were created (UNRWA 2000). Box 5.1 presents some of the key international legal standards centred on asylum and refugee status.

Box 5.1

International legal standards: defending the right to asylum

Statute of the Office of the United Nations High Commissioner for Refugees (14 December 1950)

Convention relating to the Status of Refugees (28 July 1951, into effect 22 April 1954)

Convention relating to the Status of Stateless Persons (28 September 1954, into effect 6 June 1960)

Convention on the Nationality of Married Women (29 January 1957, into effect 11 August 1958)

Protocol relating to the Status of Refugees (18 November 1966, into effect 4 October 1967)

Declaration on Territorial Asylum (14 December 1967)

Convention on the Reduction of Statelessness (30 August 1961, into effect 13 December 1975)

Declaration on the Human Rights of Individuals Who Are Not Nationals of the Country in Which They Live (13 December 1985)

For the texts of all these documents, follow the links on www.unhchr.ch

---

The 1951 Refugee Convention, in addition to basic protections of the UDHR, provides the founding statement of internationally accepted norms of refugees and asylum. Article 1 of the 1951 Refugee Convention defines a refugee as:

A person who is outside his/her country of nationality or habitual residence; has a well-founded fear of persecution because of his/her race, religion, nationality, membership in a particular social group or political opinion; and is unable or unwilling to avail himself/herself of the protection of that country, or to return there, for fear of persecution.

Defining and protecting the rights had begun with the work of the League of Nations before the Second World War. It was six years after the war, on 28 July 1951, that the United Nations approved the Convention relating to the Status of Refugees. At the beginning of the same year, the United Nations had created the High Commission for Refugees (UNHCR). The Convention defines not only the rights but the responsibilities of refugees in relation to the State in which asylum is sought. It also outlines the responsibilities of States in the protection of the rights of refugees and outlines exemptions to the Convention. War criminals, for example, do not qualify for refugee status. According to UNHCR's own figures, the Convention has helped to protect over 50 million refugees, including the 20 million it currently serves to assist.

The 1951 Convention, summarised in Box 5.2, is directed primarily at the protection of post-Second World War Europeans. A 1967 Protocol widened the focus of the Convention globally. Regionally, other instruments ensued, including the 1969 Africa Refugee Convention and the 1984 Latin American Cartagena Declaration. Today, however, especially ironically in the continental birthplace of the Convention, its contemporary appropriateness is increasingly being called into question. The UNHCR has done much work in recent years to shore up what it calls a 'timeless convention' which is now being questioned by the States that brought it into being. Yet, there is a strong defence of the Convention from official sources. Box 5.3 highlights some of the contemporary questions and concerns arising over half a century since the Convention was ratified. The 1951 Convention is a relatively long document. Box 5.2 provides a summary.

Box 5.2

Convention relating to the Status of Refugees (1951)

Chapter I is concerned with general provisions.

Article I defines a refugee as someone who 'owing to well-founded fear of being persecuted for reasons of race, religion, nationality, membership of a particular social group or political opinion' is outside the country of their nationality and who 'is unable or, owing to such fear, is unwilling' to avail him/herself 'of the protection of that country; or who, not having a nationality and being outside the country of his/her former habitual residence as a result of such events, is unable or, owing to such fear, is unwilling to return to it'. But the persons to whom the Convention refers are specifically those who are so in fear of persecution 'as a result of events occurring before 1 January 1951'. This refers to a singular,

continued

European context. 'For the purposes of this Convention, the words "events occurring before 1 January 1951" shall be understood to mean either (a) "events occurring in Europe before 1 January 1951"; or (b) "events occurring in Europe or elsewhere before 1 January 1951", and each Contracting State shall make a declaration at the time of signature, ratification or accession, specifying which of these meanings it applies for the purpose of its obligations under this Convention.' Article 1 also provides various provisos and exceptions to refugee status and entitlement to protection, including the exclusion of the protection for anyone who has 'committed a crime against peace, a war crime, or a crime against humanity, as defined in the international instruments drawn up to make provision in respect of such crimes' or 'committed a serious non-political crime outside the country of refuge prior to his admission to that country as a refugee'.

Article 2 presents obligations for the asylum seeker. 'Every refugee has duties to the country in which he finds himself, which require in particular that he conform to its laws and regulations as well as to measures taken for the maintenance of public order.'

Article 3 states that the Convention 'shall apply the provisions of this Convention to refugees without discrimination as to race, religion or country of origin'.

Article 4 outlines the obligations of Contracting States to 'accord to refugees within their territories treatment at least as favourable as that accorded to their nationals with respect to freedom to practise their religion and freedom as regards the religious education of their children'.

Article 5 is a statement of the indivisibility of human rights in that 'Nothing in this Convention shall be deemed to impair any rights and benefits granted by a Contracting State to refugees apart from this Convention.'

Article 6 defines 'in the same circumstances' as implying that any requirements (including requirements as to length and conditions of sojourn or residence) which the particular individual would *have to fulfil* for the enjoyment of the right in question, if he were not a refugee, must be fulfilled . . . with the exception of requirements which by their nature a refugee is incapable of fulfilling.

Article 7 outlines the obligations of Contracting States to provide refugees with the same basic treatment as accorded to aliens generally.

Article 8 states that, 'With regard to exceptional measures which may be taken against the person, property or interests of nationals of a foreign State, the *Contracting States shall not apply such measures to a refugee who* is formally a national of the said State solely on account of such nationality. Contracting States which, under their legislation, are prevented from applying the general principle expressed in this article, shall, in appropriate cases, grant exemptions in favour of such refugees.'

Article 9 states that, 'Nothing in this Convention shall prevent a Contracting State, in time of war or other grave and exceptional circumstances, from taking provisionally measures which it considers to be essential to the national security in the case of a particular person, pending a determination by the Contracting State that that person is in fact a refugee and that the continuance of such measures is necessary in his case in the interests of national security.'

Article 10 defines 'continuity of residence'. 'Where a refugee has been forcibly displaced during the Second World War and removed to the territory of a Contracting State, and is

continued

resident there, the period of such enforced sojourn shall be considered to have been lawful residence within that territory.'

Chapter II is concerned with juridical status.

Article 12 states that the 'personal status of a refugee shall be governed by the law of the country of his domicile or, if he has no domicile, by the law of the country of his residence'. 'Rights previously acquired by a refugee and dependent on personal status, more particularly rights attaching to marriage, shall be respected by a Contracting State.'

Article 13 deals with property rights which oblige States to accord a refugee 'treatment as favourable as possible and, in any event, not less favourable than that accorded to aliens generally in the same circumstances'. It also concerns artistic rights and industrial property and treats of 'the protection of industrial property, such as inventions, designs or models, trade marks, trade names, and of rights in literary, artistic, and scientific works'.

Article 14 states that, 'In the territory of any other Contracting State' the refugee 'shall be accorded the same protection as is accorded in that territory to nationals of the country in which he has his habitual residence'.

Article 15 deals with rights of association: 'as regards non-political and non-profit-making associations and trade unions the Contracting States shall accord to refugees lawfully staying in their territory the most favourable treatment accorded to nationals of a foreign country, in the same circumstances'.

Article 16 states that 'a refugee shall have free access to the courts of law on the territory of all Contracting States' and 'enjoy in the Contracting State in which he has his habitual residence the same treatment as a national'.

Chapter III concerns employment, including wage-earning employment (**Article 17**), self-employment (**Article 18**) and employment within the 'liberal professions' (**Article 19**).

Chapter IV concerns welfare, including access to rationing (**Article 20**), housing (**Article 21**), public education (**Article 22**), public relief (**Article 23**), labour legislation and social security (**Article 24**).

Chapter V concerns administrative measures, including the right to administrative assistance (**Article 25**), freedom of movement (**Article 26**), identity papers (**Article 27**) and travel documents (**Article 28**). It also refers to fiscal charges, and the right not to be charged higher than usual duties and taxes for nationals (**Article 29**), and guidelines on the transfer of assets (**Article 30**). It presents guidance too on refugees unlawfully in the country of refuge (**Article 31**), expulsion (**Article 32**), prohibition of expulsion or return, known as 'refoulment' (**Article 33**), and naturalisation (**Article 34**).

Chapter VI refers to 'Executory and Transitory Provisions'. This includes State obligation to co-operate with UNHCR (**Article 35**), the provision of information on national legislation (**Article 36**), and relations of the present Convention to others (**Article 37**).

Chapter VII is concerned with 'Final clauses', including the settlement of disputes (**Article 38**) and procedures for signature, ratification and accession (**Article 39**). It also refers to the 'territorial application clause' (**Article 40**), the 'federal clause' (**Article 41**), reservations (**Article 42**), entry into force (**Article 43**), denunciation (**Article 44**), revision (**Article 45**) and notifications by the Secretary-General (**Article 46**).

For the full text, follow links at www.unhcr.org

The post of UN High Commissioner for Refugees was established in 1950, a year before the 1951 Refugee Convention, the office of which is based in Geneva, Switzerland. The League of Nations had also addressed the issue of refugees but the Second World War led to a uniquely European problem of over one million displaced persons. The UN's Relief and Rehabilitation Agency and the International Refugee Organization paved the way for UNHCR, with a limited original mandate to address the problem of European refugees. As the 1951 Refugee Convention indicates in Article 1, it was only this strictly limited geographical region to which the Convention applied. According to UNHCR's own figures, in the first fifty years of its existence it has given assistance to 'at least 50 million people'. In recognition of its work, UNHCR has earned two Nobel Peace Prizes – in 1954 and 1981.

The High Commissioner reports on the results of the agency – working in 120 countries – to the Economic and Social Council. UNHCR deals today with those individuals defined as 'internally displaced persons' (IDPs) – who flee their homes but not their countries – as well as those within the stricter and more narrow definition of a person who has fled their own country into another (see Article 1). Emergency relief in times of emergency such as civil war – the major cause of IDPs – takes the form of food and water, shelter and sanitation, as well as medical welfare. In parallel to long-term and emergency relief, UNHCR has also developed the concept of 'quick impact programmes' or QIPs, which it describes as 'usually small-scale programmes to rebuild schools and clinics, repair roads, bridges and wells'. These and other such projects are 'designed to bridge the gap between emergency assistance provided to refugees and people returning home and longer-term development aid undertaken by other agencies'. Box 5.3 outlines some of the concrete ways in which UNHCR has helped refugees and internally displaced persons around the world.

Box 5.3

Where the UNHCR helps

THE BALKANS: An estimated 1.8 million civilians have returned to their home countries in the Balkans in the last few years and democratic governments, have been established in Yugoslavia and Croatia. But another 1.3 million persons remain displaced and throughout the first months of 2001 the former Yugoslav Republic of Macedonia teetered on the edge of full-scale insurrection.

COLOMBIA: Since 1985, nearly 2 million Colombians have become exiles in their own country, trying to escape a war being fought over land, ideology and drugs between Marxist guerrillas, right-wing paramilitary forces and the military. UNHCR's 2001 programme in Colombia aims at strengthening the country's ability to deal with its huge internally displaced population.

WEST AFRICA: Population movements caused by insecurity in various parts of West Africa continue throughout the region. The conflict worsened in September 2000 when parts of

continued

Guinea bordering Sierra Leone and Liberia came under attack, causing tens of thousands of Guineans and refugees to flee, and this prompted UNHCR to relocate refugees remaining in the south-western Parrot's Beak region, near the border with Sierra Leone. In the first five months of 2001, 60,000 refugees were relocated to safer camps inside Guinea.

ASYLUM IN EUROPE: Member States of the European Union have been working for several years to harmonise their asylum procedures based on the full application of the Geneva Refugee Convention. But as huge numbers of people continued to seek asylum, many governments introduced tougher laws to try to curb the flow.

CENTRAL AFRICA: Huge swathes of Central Africa remain in flames. Tanzania has the largest refugee population in Africa, mainly hosting refugees from Burundi who, at the start of 2001, were also the second largest refugee group in the world cared for by UNHCR. In May 2001, Burundi, Tanzania and UNHCR signed a tripartite agreement on the voluntary repatriation of Burundi refugees. However, the situation remains extremely volatile and the agency is not yet promoting repatriation to Burundi. In Angola, 2 million people have been uprooted, and the incessant conflicts between UNITA and the Angolan government have caused a steady number of refugee arrivals in neighbouring countries.

THE PALESTINIAN ISSUE: Around 3.8 million people are registered with the UN Relief and Works Agency (UNRWA), the organisation responsible for Palestinian refugees. Their future continues to be one of the most complex issues in the Middle East.

NORTH CAUCASUS: In August 2001, there were some 150,000 displaced persons from Chechnya living in Ingushetia. An estimated 250,000 people fled a Russian offensive in the separatist republic of Chechnya in 1999 and UNHCR and other aid agencies assisted them in surrounding republics.

AFGHANISTAN: Afghanistan has been embroiled in conflict for the last twenty-one years and, despite the return of more than 4.6 million refugees, there are still some 4 million Afghans outside their homeland, while another 750,000 people are displaced due to the civil war and drought inside the country. Afghans constitute the largest single refugee population in the world of concern to UNHCR.

SRI LANKA: UNHCR assists more than 700,000 people internally displaced by the ongoing civil conflict, after helping more than 100,000 civilians who had fled as refugees to India during the 1980s to return home.

TIMOR: Following the murder of three UNHCR aid workers in Atambua in September 2000, aid agencies withdrew from West Timor. The total number of returns since October 1999 is nearly 180,000. An estimated 100,000 East Timorese refugees remain in Indonesia. East Timor degenerated into chaos following an August 1999 vote for independence from Indonesia.

HORN OF AFRICA: In May 2001, nearly one year after an intermittent war between Ethiopia and Eritrea ended, UNHCR was able to start a major repatriation operation for the return of 174,000 long-time Eritrean refugees from neighbouring Sudan. UNHCR will implement projects to meet the immediate short-term needs of returning populations.

Further details at www.unhcr.org

Asylum through religious education: planning notes

Given the foregoing historical-legal-political background, what we need to do as religious educators is integrate the key aspects of asylum and refugee status appropriate to a religious education context. This means identifying the explicit religious context and planning for explicitly religious education learning outcomes. While presenting particular lesson plans might be prescriptive, what is offered here – adapting the structure of the QCA *Model Syllabuses for Religious Education* – is a suggested typology (Boxes 5.4.1 to 5.4.3), identifying:

* Attainment targets in religious education
* Skills and processes in religious education
* Attitudes in religious education

What follows (Box 5.4.4) is a series of suggested links for this theme to National Curriculum citizenship.

Box 5.4.1

Asylum: attainment targets in religious education

Attainment target 1: Learning about religions
Might include the ability to:
Identify, name, describe and give accounts of asylum as part of building a coherent picture of each religion

Attainment target 2: Learning from religions
Might include the ability to:
Give an informed and considered response to religious and moral issues arising from asylum, and reflect on what might be learned from religions in the light of one's own beliefs and experience

---

Box 5.4.2

Asylum: skills and processes in religious education

Investigation
Asking relevant questions about asylum and refugee status.
Balancing religious and ethical issues with pressures of nation-states in relation to immigration.
Knowing how to use different types of sources as a way of gathering information to support such investigation.

continued

Interpretation
The ability to assess critically, from religious perspectives, the range of issues raised by refugee status.

Reflection
The ability to reflect on feelings, relationships, experience, ultimate questions, beliefs and practices based upon the insecurities of life as a refugee.

Empathy
The ability to consider the thoughts, feelings, experiences, attitudes, beliefs and values of others such as refugees.

Evaluation
The ability to debate issues of religious significance with reference to evidence and argument and weighing the respective claims of self-interest, consideration for others, religious teaching and individual conscience with matters of citizenship within a nation-state.

Analysis
Distinguishing between opinion, belief and fact in assessing asylum.

Synthesis
Connecting different aspects of life into a meaningful whole, the good and the less than comfortable.

Application
Making the association between religions and individual, community, national and international life, while identifying key religious values and their interplay with secular ones, in relation to the uncertainties of refugee status.

Expression
The ability to use works of art, literature, music and theatre as sources for the creative representation and interpretation of refugee status.

Box 5.4.3

Asylum: attitudes in religious education

Commitment
Understanding the importance of commitment to a set of values by which to live one's life, even when these are challenged by difficult circumstances.

Fairness
Readiness to look beyond surface impressions and stereotypes when considering asylum.

continued

Respect
Respecting those who have different beliefs and customs, recognising the rights of others to hold their own views and the importance of avoiding ridicule, seeing that asylum seekers are often subject to such abuse.

Self-understanding
Developing the capacity to discern the personal relevance of religious questions and the value of even the stateless human being.

Enquiry
Being prepared to acknowledge bias and prejudice in oneself.
Willingness to value insight and imagination as ways of perceiving reality.

Box 5.4.4

Asylum through religious education: national curriculum citizenship links

Knowledge and understanding about becoming informed citizens
1   Pupils should be taught about:
a   the legal and human rights and responsibilities underpinning society and how they relate to citizens, including the role and operation of the criminal and civil justice systems
POSSIBLE RELIGIOUS EDUCATION LINKS: Examine the UN protection offered to refugees through the UNHCR, with a focus upon those religions being studied at a particular key stage.
b   the origins and implications of the diverse national, regional, religious and ethnic identities in the United Kingdom and the need for mutual respect and understanding
POSSIBLE RELIGIOUS EDUCATION LINKS: Religious dimensions of refugee and asylum-seeking status in local and national communities, including the positive contribution made by refugees and asylum seekers within the context of local and religious communities.
c   the work of parliament, the government and the courts in making and shaping the law
POSSIBLE RELIGIOUS EDUCATION LINKS: The work of the Home Office in supporting a plural and diverse democratic country.
f   the opportunities for individuals and voluntary groups to bring about social change locally, nationally, in Europe and internationally
POSSIBLE RELIGIOUS EDUCATION LINKS: NGOs that assist refugees such as the Refugee Council, focusing specifically on religious issues
g   the importance of a free press, and the media's role in society, including the internet, in providing information and affecting opinion
POSSIBLE RELIGIOUS EDUCATION LINKS: media portrayal of refugees and treatment of asylum-seeking issues, focusing specifically on religious issues
i   the United Kingdom's relations in Europe, including the European Union, and relations with the Commonwealth and the United Nations

continued

POSSIBLE RELIGIOUS EDUCATION LINKS: Historical and other reasons why many refugees choose the United Kingdom.

Developing skills of enquiry and communication
2   Pupils should be taught to:
a   research a topical political, spiritual, moral, social or cultural issue, problem or event by analysing information from different sources, including ICT-based sources, showing an awareness of the use and abuse of statistics
b   express, justify and defend orally and in writing a personal opinion about such issues, problems or events
c   contribute to group and exploratory class discussions, and take part in formal debates
POSSIBLE RELIGIOUS EDUCATION LINKS: See Question, discuss, research activities in Box 5.6.

Developing skills of participation and responsible action
3   Pupils should be taught to:
a   use their imagination to consider other people's experiences and be able to think about, express, explain and critically evaluate views that are not their own
b   negotiate, decide and take part responsibly in school- and community-based activities
c   reflect on the process of participating
POSSIBLE RELIGIOUS EDUCATION LINKS: See Question, discuss, research activities in Box 5.6.

In planning for citizenship through religious education, it is crucial that neither the explicit religious education nor conscious citizenship elements of delivery are lost. Box 5.5 provides the religious educator with further starting points.

Box 5.5
Asylum and refugee status resource links

United Nations High Commissioner for Refugees,
Office of the UNHCR – Geneva, Switzerland
www.unhcr.ch

Refworld
www.unhcr.ch/refworld

International Labour Organization (ILO) – Geneva, Switzerland
International Labour Standards and Human Rights
www.ilo.org

United Nations Children's Fund (UNICEF) – New York, USA
www.unicef.org

continued

Children's Rights
www.unicef.org/crc/index

The State of the World's Children 2000
www.unicef.org/sowc00/uwar2

Conclusion

Prejudice in relation to religion as well as refugee status often makes the already difficult issue of asylum seeking more complex. Box 5.6 presents a range of open-ended questions, discussion points and issues for further research. These may be used for training or, if adapted, in the classroom with pupils.

Box 5.6

Asylum through religious education:
question, discuss, research

Question and discuss

1   Do religious people have a special responsibility to care for refugees?
2   Did the 'flight into Egypt' (Matthew) make Jesus a refugee child and the son of refugees? (In a seasonal news story from December 2002, a Church of England vicar was mocked for suggesting that Jesus's family were asylum seekers.)
3   Did Mohammed's flight from Mecca to Medina make him a refugee?
4   Buddhists 'take refuge' in the three jewels: Buddha, Dharma, Sangha. What is the sense of this term 'refuge' here?
5   Post-September 11, to what extent are all refugees likely to be treated with suspicion, especially if arriving from troubled regions such as Afghanistan or Iraq? (For more information on changing attitudes towards refugees, post-September 11, see www.hrw.org)
6   Do religious educators have a particular role to play in the education of refugees?

Research

7   Visit the Home Office website at www.homeoffice.gov.uk
    A major responsibility of the Home Office as part of the UK government is to maintain policy and establish controls in regard to immigration. Follow links to the immigration document 'Secure Borders, Safe Haven: Integration with Diversity in Modern Britain'. Does this document take seriously the issue of religious diversity?
8   For views on UK government policy on immigration, asylum seekers and refugees, see the Refugee Council site at www.therefugeecouncil.org.uk. Use this Refugee Council

continued

---

website to collect religious education-relevant resources (these will be highlighted on the website under education).

9   Visit the website of the UN High Commissioner for Refugees at www.unhcr.org. Access the full document of the 1951 Refugee Convention. In the Annexes to this document, you will find copies of the sort of documentation refugees need while in transition. To what extent is religious or cultural identity a feature?

Chapter 6

Slavery through religious education

Introduction

Slavery is one of those peculiarly despicable practices that remained in the sidelines of an ancient world Mediterranean that prided itself as the source of democracy (Shaw 2001). Slavery was similarly prevalent in first-century Christianity where references to the practice are common – and largely uncondemned – throughout the New Testament. It was a given of early Christianity (Glancy 2001). Slavery was an historical reality through the centuries after the first and second centuries of the Christian era, with an extensive literature charting its different social, political and historical incarnations (Engerman *et al.* 2000; Harmer 2001, Tackach 2001; Rohrbach 2002). It was also a practice that continued to be justified by Christianity until recent centuries (Davis 2001; Haynes 2002). Debates over the past decade or so have raised the spectre of reparation for the historical injustices of slavery, especially from America where only the Civil War ended slavery with emancipation (Horowitz 2002), and Britain in the history of Empire (Walvin 2001).

Slavery takes many different guises and yet is a difficult state to define. As such, it is sometimes concealed behind supposed norms of traditional societies. For religious educators, slavery remains an issue on a number of fundamental levels: a matter of the most basic freedom, an issue of economic exploitation, an historical phenomenon that religious traditions themselves justified and benefited from, and, where caste means deprivation of human dignity, an ingrained part of the *present-day*, social and cultural life experience of around 250 million people today through the caste system (Gearon 2002).

Slavery: historical-legal-political background

The United Nations (2002f) *Fact Sheet on Modern Slavery* demonstrates clearly that slavery is far from a defunct practice. Scholars such as Bales (2000) have made estimates of the number of modern slaves in tens of millions, arguably in excess of slave populations in any time of world history (cf. Shepherd 2002). The issue of modern slavery retains the major characteristics of its historical antecedents: exploitation, the absence of freedom, compulsion – whether this is forced labour such as that reported in the 2001 Report of the Important Eminent Persons Group on *Slavery, Abduction and Forced Servitude in Sudan* or the trafficking of women and children for sexual and economic exploitation, as in the Washington-based Protection Project and its *Country-by-Country Report on a Contemporary Form of Slavery* (Nitze 2002).

The preamble to the Universal Declaration of Human Rights is a discourse on the fundamental freedoms. Enslavement of human beings in any form is therefore anathema to and incompatible with any notion of human rights. The Universal Declaration begins in Article 1 with the fundamental statement that, 'All human beings are born free and equal in dignity and rights.'

According to the United Nations:

> the word slavery today covers a variety of human rights violations. In addition to traditional slavery and the slave trade, these abuses include the sale of children, child prostitution, child pornography, the exploitation of child labour, the sexual mutilation of female children, the use of children in armed conflicts, debt bondage, the traffic in persons and in the sale of human organs, the exploitation of prostitution, and certain practices under apartheid and colonial régimes.

Slavery may be formally prohibited by the 1948 Universal Declaration of Human Rights (Article 4), by the 1956 UN Supplementary Convention on the Abolition of Slavery, the Slave Trade and Institutions and Practices Similar to Slavery, and a range of other international standards.

The world's leading and longest-standing organisation working specifically on slavery suggests that when people think of slavery, an image of the past is conjured up. Anti-Slavery International defines slavery by a number of common characteristics distinguishing slavery from other human rights violations. A slave is:
* Forced to work through mental or physical threat;
* Owned or controlled by an 'employer', usually through mental or physical abuse or threatened abuse;
* Dehumanised, treated as a commodity or bought and sold as 'property';
* Physically constrained or has restrictions placed on his/her freedom of movement.

Forms of slavery existing today are described below.

* Bonded labour affects at least 20 million people around the world. People become bonded labourers by taking or being tricked into taking a loan for as little as the cost of medicine for a sick child. To repay the debt, they are forced to work long hours, seven days a week, 365 days a year. They receive basic food and shelter as 'payment' for their work, but may never pay off the loan, which can be passed down through several generations.
* Forced labour affects people who are illegally recruited by governments, political parties or private individuals, and forced to work – usually under threat of violence or other penalties.

- Worst forms of child labour refers to children who work in exploitative or dangerous conditions. Tens of millions of children around the world work full-time, depriving them of the education and recreation crucial to their personal and social development.
- Commercial sexual exploitation of children. Children are exploited for their commercial value through prostitution, trafficking and pornography. They are often kidnapped, bought, or forced to enter the sex market.
- Trafficking involves the transport and/or trade of humans, usually women or children, for economic gain using force or deception. Often migrant women are tricked and forced into domestic work or prostitution.
- Early and forced marriage affects women and girls who are married without choice and are forced into lives of servitude often accompanied by physical violence.
- Traditional or 'chattel' slavery involves the buying and selling of people. They are often abducted from their homes, inherited or given as gifts.

(Anti-Slavery International 2002, visit www.asi.org.uk)

A practice embedded into almost all supposedly civilised ancient societies, from the days of the abolitionists slavery was arguably amongst the first 'human rights' issues to attract international protest at something which was clearly an infringement of human dignity and liberty. While different countries have in recent centuries made the practice illegal, international efforts to outlaw slavery date to the late nineteenth and early twentieth centuries. Such moves included the 1889-90 General Act of Brussels Conference (aimed specifically at ending traffic in African slaves) and the 1919 Convention of Saint-Germain-en-Laye (revising the 1885 General Act of Berlin and the 1890 Declaration of Brussels). These attempts to suppress slavery in all its forms and banish the slave trade from land and sea were taken up by the League of Nations' Temporary Slavery Commission (appointed in 1924). The 1926 Slavery Convention (which entered into force in 1927) remains today the foundation for international standards set by the United Nations (see Boxes 6.1 and 6.2). Later documents include the Protocol amending the Slavery Convention (1953) and the Supplementary Convention on the Abolition of Slavery, the Slave Trade, and Institutions and Practices Similar to Slavery (1956). Indeed, these two documents consist of many statements that simply replace references to the League of Nations with the United Nations.

Box 6.1

International legal standards: defending against slavery

Slavery Convention (25 September 1926, into effect 9 March 1927)
Forced Labour Convention (28 June 1930, into effect 1 May 1932)

continued

Convention for the Suppression of the Traffic in Persons and of the Exploitation of the Prostitution of Others (2 December 1949, into effect 25 July 1951)
Protocol amending the Slavery Convention (23 October 1953, into effect 7 December 1953)
Supplementary Convention on the Abolition of Slavery, the Slave Trade, and Institutions and Practices Similar to Slavery (30 April 1956/7 September 1956, into effect 30 April 1957)
Abolition of Forced Labour Convention (25 June 1957, into effect 17 January 1959)

For full texts, follow links to www.un.unhchr.org

Box 6.2
Slavery Convention
25 September 1926, into effect 9 March 1927

Article 1 states that, for the purpose of the Convention, 'the following definitions are agreed upon:
(1) Slavery is the status or condition of a person over whom any or all of the powers attaching to the right of ownership are exercised.
(2) The slave trade includes all acts involved in the capture, acquisition or disposal of a person with intent to reduce him to slavery; all acts involved in the acquisition of a slave with a view to selling or exchanging him; all acts of disposal by sale or exchange of a slave acquired with a view to being sold or exchanged, and, in general, every act of trade or transport in slaves.'
Article 2 commits the contracting parties of the League of Nations' 'each in respect of the territories placed under its sovereignty, jurisdiction, protection, suzerainty or tutelage, so far as they have not already taken the necessary steps:
(a) To prevent and suppress the slave trade;
(b) To bring about, progressively and as soon as possible, the complete abolition of slavery in all its forms.'
Article 3 commits contracting parties to 'undertake to adopt all appropriate measures with a view to preventing and suppressing the embarkation, disembarkation and transport of slaves in their territorial waters and upon all vessels flying their respective flags.'
Article 4 commits contracting parties to 'give to one another every assistance with the object of securing the abolition of slavery and the slave trade'.
Article 5 commits contracting parties to recognising 'that recourse to compulsory or forced labour may have grave consequences and undertake, each in respect of the territories placed under its sovereignty, jurisdiction, protection, suzerainty or tutelage, to take all necessary measures to prevent compulsory or forced labour from developing into conditions analogous to slavery'.
Article 6 commits contracting parties 'whose laws do not at present make adequate provision for the punishment of infractions of laws and regulations enacted with a view to giving effect to the purposes of the present Convention' to 'undertake to adopt the necessary measures in order that severe penalties may be imposed in respect of such infractions'.

continued

Article 7 commits contracting parties 'to communicate to each other and to the Secretary-General of the League of Nations any laws and regulations which they may enact with a view to the application of the provisions of the present Convention'.

Article 8 commits contracting parties to 'agree that disputes arising between them relating to the interpretation or application of this Convention shall, if they cannot be settled by direct negotiation, be referred for decision to the Permanent Court of International Justice'.

Article 9 concerns the implications for contracting parties of signing or ratifying the Convention, and the nature of the legal obligations across its territories.

Article 10 concerns the denunciation of the Convention, and the procedures and implications of this.

Article 11 concerns procedures for signing the Convention, 'open for signature by the States Members of the League of Nations until April 1st, 1927', when the Secretary-General of the League of Nations 'will subsequently bring the present Convention to the notice of States which have not signed it, including States which are not Members of the League of Nations, and invite them to accede thereto'.

Article 12 concerns the ratification and operational status of the Convention.

For the full text of the document, follow links at www.unhchr.org

Slavery through religious education: planning notes

Given the foregoing historical-legal-political grounding, what we need to do as religious educators is integrate the key aspects of slavery appropriate to a religious education context. This means identifying the explicit religious context and planning for explicitly religious education learning outcomes.

While presenting particular lesson plans might be prescriptive, what is offered here – adapting the structure of the QCA *Model Syllabuses for Religious Education* – is a suggested typology (Boxes 6.3.1 to 6.3.3), identifying:

- Attainment targets in religious education
- Skills and processes in religious education
- Attitudes in religious education

What follows (Box 6.3.4) is a series of suggested links for this theme to National Curriculum citizenship.

Box 6.3.1

Slavery: attainment targets in religious education

Attainment target 1: Learning about religions
Identify a critical period in the history of slavery and give an account of the cultural, ethnic and/or religious involvement.

continued

Explore religious language, stories and symbolism which narrate the abuses of and liberation from slavery.

Attainment target 2: Learning from religions
Give an informed and considered response to the religious and moral issues surrounding slavery.
Reflect on freedom as the fundamental human right and the limitations of such freedom.
Identify and respond to questions of meaning with which slavery confronts humanity.

Box 6.3.2

Slavery: skills and processes in religious education

Investigation
Knowing how to use different types of sources as a way of gathering information about slavery and what may constitute evidence for understanding religions and their participation in or status as victims of slavery.

Interpretation
The ability to draw from artefacts, works of art, poetry and symbolism reflecting the condition of the slave through the centuries as well as moments of liberation.

Reflection
The ability to reflect on feelings, relationships, experience, ultimate questions, beliefs and practices in the face of slavery.

Empathy
The ability to consider the thoughts, feelings, experiences, attitudes, beliefs and values of others who have suffered from enslavement in all its forms through history and today.

Evaluation
The ability to debate issues of religious significance with reference to evidence of slavery and especially its tolerance by religious traditions or even its theological justification.

Analysis
Distinguishing between opinion, belief and fact in relation to slavery.

Synthesis
Linking significant features of religious attitudes to slavery over the centuries and linking the paradoxes together in a coherent pattern.

Application
Making the association between religions and individual, community, national and

continued

international life, identifying key religious values and their interplay with secular ones, especially in the role of NGOs in campaigning against the slave trade.

Expression
The ability to identify and articulate matters of deep conviction and concern, and respond to religious questions through a variety of media – art, music, the novel – in relation to slavery and the slave trade.

Box 6.3.3

Slavery: attitudes in religious education

Commitment
Understanding the importance of commitment to a set of values by which to live one's life, often against all reason for hope.

Fairness
Considering the fundamental injustices of slavery and the slave trade.

Respect
Learning discernment of what is worthy of respect and what is not.

Self-understanding
Developing a mature sense of self-worth and value; developing the capacity to discern the personal relevance of religious questions.

Enquiry
Investigate why slavery persists today.

Box 6.3.4

Slavery through religious education: National Curriculum citizenship links

Knowledge and understanding about becoming informed citizens
1   Pupils should be taught about:
a   the legal and human rights and responsibilities underpinning society and how they relate to citizens, including the role and operation of the criminal and civil justice systems POSSIBLE RELIGIOUS EDUCATION LINKS: Moral and ethical issues raised by questions of freedom and slavery from secular (for example, UN) and theological/philosophical perspectives.

continued

b   the origins and implications of the diverse national, regional, religious and ethnic identities in the United Kingdom and the need for mutual respect and understanding
    POSSIBLE RELIGIOUS EDUCATION LINKS: Colonial and slave histories in communities within the United Kingdom and how present-day religious communities regard and answer for such histories

e   how the economy functions, including the role of business and financial services

f   the opportunities for individuals and voluntary groups to bring about social change locally, nationally, in Europe and internationally
    POSSIBLE RELIGIOUS EDUCATION LINKS (for e and f): Treatment of the ethical issues raised by modern 'slavery' and how religiously-based NGOs campaign against such practices (see also j below).

i   the United Kingdom's relations in Europe, including the European Union, and relations with the Commonwealth and the United Nations
    POSSIBLE RELIGIOUS EDUCATION LINKS: Colonial and Commonwealth relations today, particularly pluralism and diversity of culture and religion as a source of enrichment and conflict.

j   the wider issues and challenges of global interdependence and responsibility, including sustainable development and Local Agenda 21 (see e and f above)

Developing skills of enquiry and communication

2   Pupils should be taught to:

a   research a topical political, spiritual, moral, social or cultural issue, problem or event by analysing information from different sources, including ICT-based sources, showing an awareness of the use and abuse of statistics

b   express, justify and defend orally and in writing a personal opinion about such issues, problems or events

c   contribute to group and exploratory class discussions, and take part in formal debates
POSSIBLE RELIGIOUS EDUCATION LINKS: See Question, discuss, research activities in Box 6.4.

Developing skills of participation and responsible action

3   Pupils should be taught to:

a   use their imagination to consider other people's experiences and be able to think about, express, explain and critically evaluate views that are not their own

b   negotiate, decide and take part responsibly in school- and community-based activities

c   reflect on the process of participating
POSSIBLE RELIGIOUS EDUCATION LINKS: See Question, discuss, research activities in Box 6.4.

Conclusion

For religious educators, slavery remains an issue on a number of fundamental levels. Good teaching always prepares the learner for a yearning to know more or question further. Box 6.4 raises some of the questions opened up by this chapter on slavery through religious education.

Box 6.4

Slavery through religious education: question, discuss, research

Question and discuss

1 According to the Jewish Torah, the Israelites were slaves in Egypt. The Jewish Passover is a powerful ceremony of liberation from slavery in the broadest sense. What does freedom mean in the context of modern Jewish history?

2 The New Testament has numerous references to slavery, none of them condemnatory of the practice. How can we interpret this today?

3 Are modern forms of slavery different in kind or quality from the image of slavery inherited from the history books?

4 Slavery in this book is classified as an infringement of civil and political rights. To what extent is modern slavery more a form of economic exploitation rather than slavery 'proper'?

5 What pressure can a religious person exert against slavery? For instance, given what we know about 'slave labour' in the production of chocolate, should a religious person not eat chocolate out of conscience?

6 One of St Paul's letters, the shortest one he ever wrote, is written to Philemon, a slave. Read Paul's letter and discuss Paul's attitude to Philemon in terms of personal and social status.

7 Can caste in religious traditions such as Hinduism be described as a sort of institutionalised slavery?

Research

8 Visit the website of Human Rights Watch (HRW) at www.hrw.org Find out what you can about HRW's campaigns against the trafficking of women for prostitution.

9 Visit one of the websites of Christian Aid or Cafod. Find out about their campaigns against child labour.

10 Anti-Slavery International is one of the world's largest and most established pressure groups against slavery. Visit its website at www.asi.org

Chapter 7

Freedom of expression through religious education

Introduction

Suppression and censorship for religious reasons occur in liberal democracies as well as States dominated by religious interests (UN 2002b). With the seeming preoccupation with toleration and conciliation without restriction, religious suppression and outright censorship (where religious forces are supported by the power of the State) are examples of the heightened tension between the notion of universal rights promulgated by the international community through the United Nations and more 'local' culturally particular and especially religious contexts.

Freedom of expression: historical-legal-political background

The human rights context is fundamentally that of the UN's 1948 Universal Declaration of Human Rights. The theme centres around the protection of freedom of thought, conscience and religion (Article 18) and freedom of opinion and expression, including the 'freedom to hold opinions without interference and to seek, receive and impart information and ideas through any media and regardless of frontiers' (Article 19). Subsequent Declarations, Covenants and Conventions provide varying degrees of legal status for the protection of these and related rights, including:

- Convention on the International Rights of Correction (1952)
- International Covenant on Civil and Political Rights (1996)
- International Covenant on Social, Economic and Cultural Rights (1966)
- United Nations Declaration on the Elimination of All Forms of Intolerance and Discrimination Based on Religion or Belief (1981)
- United Nations Declaration on the Rights of Persons Belonging to National or Ethnic, Religious, and Linguistic Minorities (1992)
- The Cairo Declaration on Human Rights in Islam (1990)
- Vienna Declaration and Plan of Action (1993)
- Oslo Declaration on Freedom of Religion and Belief (1998)

- World Conference Against Racism, Xenophobia and Related Forms of Discrimination (2002)

Censorship and suppression of artistic expression (in the widest sense) is yet another example of where religious traditions have not been guardians of (here cultural) rights. Today there may be remaining contradictions between so-called universal rights and religious traditions – what Huntington (1993) famously described as a 'Clash of Civilizations'. Yet, it is a worthy reminder, as we shall note, that clashes between, say, religious values and fundamental rights to freedom of expression can also surface within liberal, western democracies supposedly founded upon the principles of basic rights and freedoms. Two celebrated mainstream and high-profile media cases of writers variously condemned by religious groups include Salman Rushdie and J.K. Rowling. The cases are not an exact parallel – the Harry Potter books have not suffered the same level of direct repression and banning as Rushdie's work – but both raise interesting questions from two different traditions. They are also a worthy reminder, as intimated and without prejudice to views of either side, that even in a western liberal democracy and the supposed heartland of rights discourse the force of religious views can be contrary to a prevailing rights culture.

Satanic Verses was first banned in 1988 in India after protests by Muslim groups. Since then it has been banned in South Africa, Pakistan, Saudi Arabia, Egypt, Somalia, Bangladesh, Sudan, Malaysia, Indonesia, Qatar, Papua New Guinea, Thailand, Sri Lanka, Kenya, Tanzania, Liberia, Sierra Leone, Venezuela, Bulgaria, Poland and Japan. On 12 February 1989 the Ayatollah Khomeini of Iran issued a fatwa against Salman Rushdie, which was reconfirmed by the Iranian government after the Ayatollah's death. A Muslim charity offered $6 million dollars for Salman Rushdie's death. Rushdie was forced into hiding with the protection of the British government. The latter cut off diplomatic links with Iran. Attempts to sell the book in different parts of the world were met with violence and bloodshed, including the firebombing of bookshops in Britain. Assassination attempts have been made against several translators of *Satanic Verses*.

According to the American Library Association's Office for Intellectual Freedom, the Harry Potter books headed their 'most challenged' books list for three years running, from 1999 to 2001. In 1999, they reached the top of the list, with twenty-six challenges to remove them from the shelves of libraries in twenty-six states. By 2000, Harry Potter books were placed among the top one hundred most challenged books of the decade. In January 2001, it was reported that the number of complaints against Harry Potter books in the USA had tripled since 1999. On 29 March 2000, Revd George Bender of the Harvest Assembly of God Church, Pennsylvania, USA, led a ceremonial burning of a Harry Potter book. On 30 December 2001, Revd John Brock of the Christ Community Church, Alamogordo, New Mexico, led a book-burning service in which Harry Potter and other books were thrown into the flames. In November 2001, the United States Conference of Catholic Bishops issued a statement about the Stone film of Harry Potter: 'Parents concerned about the film's sorcery element should know that it is unlikely to pose any threat to Catholic beliefs. Harry Potter is so obviously innocuous fantasy that its fiction is easily distinguishable from life.' Attempted and implemented censorship of the above sort has also been evident from several other countries. The list includes the UK (St Mary's School, Chatham, Kent), Australia (the Christian Outreach College, Queensland, and about sixty Seventh Day Adventist schools), Canada (the Durham Region School Board and others), Germany (schools in the Muensingen-Reitheim district), the United Arab Emirates (all private schools), and Taiwan (the Ling-Leung Church).

One of the longest established NGOs concerned with freedom of expression is International PEN (Poets, Essayists, Novelists). Truly global in scope, it rightly describes itself as a 'worldwide association of writers'. The organisation has three guiding principles:

- To promote intellectual co-operation and understanding among writers.
- To create a world community of writers that would emphasise the central role of literature in the development of world culture.
- To defend literature against the many threats to its survival that the modern world poses.

The PEN Charter is based on resolutions passed at its International Congresses and may be summarised as follows:

PEN affirms that:
1 Literature, national though it be in origin, knows no frontiers, and should remain common currency between nations in spite of political or international upheavals.
2 In all circumstances, and particularly in time of war, works of art, the patrimony of humanity at large, should be left untouched by national or political passion.
3 Members of PEN should at all times use what influence they have in favour of good understanding and mutual respect between nations; they pledge themselves to do their utmost to dispel race, class and national hatreds, and to champion the ideal of one humanity living in peace in one world.
4 PEN stands for the principle of unhampered transmission of thought within each nation and between all nations, and members pledge themselves to oppose any form of suppression of freedom of expression in the country and community to which they belong, as well as throughout the world wherever this is possible. PEN declares for a free press and opposes arbitrary censorship in time of peace. It believes that the necessary advance of the world towards a more highly organised political and economic order renders a free criticism of governments, administrations and institutions imperative. And since freedom implies voluntary restraint, members pledge themselves to oppose such evils of a free press as mendacious publication, deliberate falsehood and distortion of facts for political and personal ends. Membership of PEN is open to all qualified writers, editors and translators who subscribe to these aims, without regard to nationality, language, race, colour or religion.

PEN operates three programmes, organising its work around: exiled writers, writers for peace and writers in prison.

Beyond the arts, which often are the only force to offer challenge to dictatorships when mass media is in state control, the Index on Censorship calling this work the 'embarrassment of tyrannies' (Webb and Bell 1997), repression of media is still a serious issue in many countries of the world. Far from being a luxury, freedom of artistic and journalistic expression – the two are closely related – is foundational to democracies, and anathema to dictatorships. Box 7.1 highlights some international legal standards affecting the media, the arts and freedom of expression.

Box 7.1

International legal standards: defending freedom of expression

Convention on the International Right of Correction (16 December 1952, into effect 24 August 1962)
Covenant on Civil and Political Rights (1966)
International Covenant on Social, Economic and Cultural Rights (1966)
Declaration of the Principles of International Cultural Co-operation (UNESCO) (4 November 1966)
Recommendation concerning Education for International Understanding, Co-operation and Peace and Education relating to Human Rights and Fundamental Freedoms (UNESCO) (19 November 1974)

For full texts of the documents, follow links at www.unhchr.org

---

Box 7.2 presents the religious educator with a wealth of potential sources for use in the classroom or for professional development, with links through the United Nations Educational, Scientific and Cultural Organization (UNESCO); and Box 7.2 provides a list of links to wider aspects of censorship and the repression of free expression.

Box 7.2

UNESCO links

United Nations Educational, Scientific and Cultural Organization (UNESCO) – Paris, France
www.unesco.org

Division of Human Rights, Democracy, Peace & Tolerance
www.unesco.org/human_rights/index

continued

Management of Social Transformations Programme (MOST)
www.unesco.org/most

Multiculturalism
www.unesco.org/most/most1

Linguistic rights
www.unesco.org/most/ln1

Religious rights
www.unesco.org/most/rr1

Cultural heritage
www.unesco.org/culture/heritage

Intercultural dialogue and pluralism
www.unesco.org/culture/dial_eng

World Intellectual Property Organization (WIPO) – Geneva, Switzerland
www.wipo.int

Traditional Knowledge
www.wipo.org/traditionalknowledge/introduction/index

Universal Declaration on Linguistic Rights
www.troc.es/ciemen/mercator

Child Rights
www.unicef.org/crc/index

The State of the World's Children 2000
www.unicef.org/sowc00/uwar2

World Education Forum: Dakar 2000
www.unicef.org/efa/results

For full texts of the documents, follow links at www.unhchr.org

---

Box 7.3

More general links to literary censorship

Index on Censorship
www.index.org

Charter '88
www.charter88.org

Human Rights Watch
www.hrw.org

Links to the Hellman-Hammett Awards and through world reports to 'Freedom of Expression on the Internet'

Global Internet Liberty Campaign (GILC)
www.gilc.org

Council of Europe Cybercrime Treaty
www.conventions.coe.int/Treaty/EN/projets/FinalCybercrime

Oxford Internet Institute
www.ox.oii

Freedom of expression through religious education: planning notes

Given the foregoing historical-legal-political grounding, what we need to do as religious educators is integrate the key aspects of freedom of expression appropriate to a religious education context. This means identifying the explicit religious context and planning for explicitly religious education learning outcomes.

While presenting particular lesson plans might be prescriptive, what is offered here – adapting the structure of the QCA *Model Syllabuses for Religious Education* – is a suggested typology (Boxes 7.4.1 to 7.4.3), identifying:

* Attainment targets in religious education
* Skills and processes in religious education
* Attitudes in religious education

What follows (Box 7.4.4) is a series of suggested links for this theme to National Curriculum citizenship.

Box 7.4.1

Freedom of expression: attainment targets in religious education

Attainment target 1: Learning about religions

Identify critical issues in the human right of freedom of expression and how religious believers are often at the heart of controversies over censorship.

Explore religious language, stories and symbolism that have been censored or repressed and the religious reasons for this.

Attainment target 2: Learning from religions

Give an informed and considered response to the religious and moral issues surrounding issues of censorship and sensitivity to deeply held beliefs of the religious person.

Box 7.4.2

Freedom of expression: skills and processes in religious education

Investigation

Asking relevant questions about freedom of expression and identifying its main manifestations – from the arts to journalism.

Knowing how to use different types of sources as a way of gathering information about freedom of expression and what may constitute evidence for understanding religions and their participation in or status as victims of censorship.

Interpretation

The ability to draw from artefacts, works of art, poetry and symbolism reflecting challenges to and justifications for freedom of expression.

Reflection

The ability to reflect on feelings, relationships, experience, ultimate questions, beliefs and practices in the face of freedom of expression and whether there can ever be limits to this.

Empathy

The ability to consider the justifications for and implications of different forms of censorship – from the arts to journalism – and the ambivalent religious role in such.

Evaluation

The ability to debate issues of religious significance with reference to evidence and argument on freedom of expression.

continued

Analysis
Distinguishing between opinion, belief and fact, especially in assessments of propaganda, from or against religious sources.

Synthesis
Linking significant features of religion together in a coherent pattern – the role of a tension between expression and repression?

Application
Making the association between religions and individual, community, national and international life, identifying key religious values and their interplay with secular ones, especially in the role of NGOs.

Expression
The ability to identify and articulate matters of deep conviction and concern, their expression through a variety of sacred and secular forms – art, music, the novel – and their survival despite repression.

Box 7.4.3

Freedom of expression: attitudes in religious education

Commitment
Understanding the importance of commitment to a set of values by which to live one's life, and the courage of the artist and writer against tyranny and repression.

Fairness
A willingness to consider evidence and argument in the face of repression, including an honest appraisal of whether censoring or banning can ever be justified.

Respect
Recognising the rights of others to hold their own views; the avoidance of ridicule; and the discernment of what is worthy of respect and what is not.

Self-understanding
Developing a mature sense of self-worth and value, developing the capacity to discern the personal relevance of religious questions in relation to freedom of expression.

Enquiry
Curiosity and a desire to seek the truth in a variety of religious and secular forms.

Box 7.4.4

Freedom of expression through religious education: National Curriculum citizenship links

Knowledge and understanding about becoming informed citizens

I Pupils should be taught about:

f the opportunities for individuals and voluntary groups to bring about social change locally, nationally, in Europe and internationally

g the importance of a free press, and the media's role in society, including the internet, in providing information and affecting opinion

POSSIBLE RELIGIOUS EDUCATION LINKS: The work of NGOs and government bodies involved with censorship, including censorship for religious reasons.

Developing skills of enquiry and communication

2 Pupils should be taught to:

a research a topical political, spiritual, moral, social or cultural issue, problem or event by analysing information from different sources, including ICT-based sources, showing an awareness of the use and abuse of statistics

b express, justify and defend orally and in writing a personal opinion about such issues, problems or events

c contribute to group and exploratory class discussions, and take part in formal debates

POSSIBLE RELIGIOUS EDUCATION LINKS: See Question, discuss, research activities in Box 7.5

Developing skills of participation and responsible action

3 Pupils should be taught to:

a use their imagination to consider other people's experiences and be able to think about, express, explain and critically evaluate views that are not their own

b negotiate, decide and take part responsibly in school- and community-based activities

c reflect on the process of participating

POSSIBLE RELIGIOUS EDUCATION LINKS: See Question, discuss, research activities in Box 7.5.

Conclusion

When people in the world are hungry or acts of genocide are being perpetrated, the right to express oneself may not seem to rate very highly on the scale of rights for the citizen. But freedom of expression, the right to express an opinion or a view without fear of harassment or punishment, is often a gauge to other threats to liberty and democracy. A government that stops journalists from reporting, writers from telling stories or readers from buying books which contain challenging ideas will often indicate a regime or an ideology, or even a religion, that is less than tolerant of other rights of the citizen. The fatwa against Salman Rushdie prefaced more deadly threats a decade later. Box 7.5 provides a range of points for question and discussion.

Box 7.5

Freedom of expression through religious education: question, discuss, research

Question and discuss

1   Is it ever right for religious traditions to ban books because they cause offence?
2   Some of the links between religion and literary censorship have attracted substantial systematic enquiry, but there is little comparative analysis (from two or more religious perspectives), even less that tries to gauge the role of the media. Why does religious education always seem to avoid the really controversial issues?
3   In relation to matters of 'freedom of thought, conscience and religion' and 'freedom of opinion and expression', the media representation of Rushdie and Rowling has been central to public debate on supposedly universal 'norms', with the international media itself subject to and a vehicle of censorship. What patterns are there in the responses to the censorship of Rushdie and Rowling in the UK and (selected) international media and how effective have attempts here been to support, mitigate or counteract such censorship?
4   What is the specific religious-ideological (especially Islamic/Christian theological) thinking behind and historical context of the censorship of these two British writers? Are there any fundamental differences (theological, political, and so forth) in Islamic and Christian justification for literary repression between and within the traditions?
5   Do these two high-profile case studies provide emergent paradigms for the analysis of writers censored in particular for religious reasons?
6   What should be the media's role in representing censorship – attack, defence or advocacy?
7   Does the defence of an author who is read by a minority but offends the majority matter? Does the defence of an author who is read by a majority but offends a 'minority' matter?
8   The relationship between religion and art is a popular topic in schools at all levels and provides immense possibilities for exploring how religious traditions culturally express philosophical and theological truths. Examining the history of iconoclasm within Christianity, especially the destruction of religious images during some of the bloody times in the post-Reformation period, what does this tell us about the history of the relationship between religion and the visual arts?
9   Two much discussed and publicised cases of censorship are Salman Rushdie's *Satanic Verses* and the banning of J.K. Rowling's *Harry Potter* books. These books highlight the complex relationship between:
   a   literary censorship at the level of the state or public institutions impelled by religious motives
   b   the principles that religious authorities adhere to in advocating censorship
   c   the mass media role in representing literary censorship on religious grounds
   Is religiously grounded literary censorship ever justifiable?

continued

Research

10   Literature suppressed on religious grounds includes (very selectively) the following:
The Age of Reason Thomas Paine
Children of the Alley Naguib Mahfouz
Christianity Restored Michael Servetus
Church: Charism and Power: Liberation Theology and the Institutional Church Leonardo Boff
Dialogue Concerning the Two Chief World Systems Galileo Galilei
Essays Michael Montaigne
The Guide of the Perplexed Moses Maimonides
The Hidden Face of Eve: Women in the Arab World Nawal El Sadawi
Infallible? An Inquiry Hans Kung
Lajja (Shame) Taslima Nasrin
The Last Temptation of Christ Nikos Kazantzakis
The New Testament trans. William Tyndale
Ninety-Five Theses Martin Luther
Oliver Twist Charles Dickens
On the Infinite Universe and Worlds Giordano Bruno
On the Origin of Species Charles Darwin
Harry Potter and The Philosopher's Stone J.K. Rowling
The Red and the Black Stendhal (Marie Henri Beyle)
Religion within the Limits of Reason Alone Immanuel Kant
The Satanic Verses Salman Rushdie
The Sorrows of Young Werther Johann Wolfgang von Goethe

(Adapted from Karolides *et al.* 1999)

There is considerable value in developing academic and public understanding of the media representation of religion in social and political context. What can religious educationalists do to assist the process? In school, what opportunities are there for collaboration with departments of art, drama and English?

Chapter 8

Freedom of religion and belief through religious education

Introduction

For religious educators in the UK and the children they teach, freedom to practise a religion of their choice is a given. The right to hold no religious beliefs is also seen as a basic right of the citizen. This chapter examines some of the background to the right of religious freedom and belief, suggesting some ways in which it might be incorporated into religious education.

Freedom of religion and belief: historical-legal-political background

The Universal Declaration of Human Rights includes a number of articles of relevance to freedom of religion and belief. These include Article 2 (forbidding prejudicial distinctions of any kind, including those related to religion), Article 26 (on the rights to a particular religious education) and Article 29 (on responsibilities and proscription against limitations of proclaimed rights). The foundation stone of freedom of religion and belief, though, is to be found in Article 18 of the Universal Declaration of Human Rights. This states that:

> Everyone has the right to freedom of: thought, conscience and religion; this right includes freedom to change his religion or belief, and freedom, either alone or in community with others and in public or private, to manifest his religion or belief in teaching, practice, worship and observance.

A selective list of other, relevant international standards is presented in Box 8.1.

The preamble to the UN Declaration on the Elimination of All Forms of Intolerance and of Discrimination Based on Religion or Belief (1981; cf. UN 2002f) restates the wider context of the Charter of the UN. Notably this reiterates the 'dignity and equality inherent in all human beings', international commitment on the promotion of universal human rights and fundamental freedoms for all, 'without distinction as to race, sex, language or religion', and the principles of non-discrimination and equality before the law

---

Box 8.1

International legal standards: defending freedom of religion and belief

Declaration on the Elimination of All Forms of Intolerance and of Discrimination Based on Religion or Belief (25 November 1981)
Declaration on the Rights of Persons Belonging to National or Ethnic, Religious and Linguistic Minorities (18 December 1992)
Oslo Declaration on Freedom of Religion and Belief (1998)
World Conference Against Racism, Xenophobia and Related Forms of Discrimination (September 2002)

For a full text of the document, follow links at www.unhchr.org

---

and the right to freedom of thought, conscience, religion and belief. As with the Convention on the International Rights of Correction, the UN Declaration on the Elimination of All Forms of Intolerance and of Discrimination Based on Religion or Belief also emphasises the role of such freedoms in the maintenance of a stable international order:

> Considering that the disregard and infringement of human rights and fundamental freedoms, in particular of the right to freedom of thought, conscience, religion or whatever belief, have brought, directly or indirectly, wars and great suffering to mankind, especially where they serve as a means of foreign interference in the internal affairs of other States and amount to kindling hatred between peoples and nations.

In addition, 'freedom of religion and belief should also contribute to the attainment of the goals of world peace, social justice and friendship among peoples and to the elimination of ideologies or practices of colonialism and racial discrimination'. All this somewhat supports our preliminary analysis of the importance of colonial and postcolonial relations between nations as being of paramount importance. But the 1981 Declaration is also concerned by 'manifestations of intolerance and by the existence of discrimination in matters of religion or belief still in evidence in some areas of the world'. The 1981 Declaration (see Box 8.2 for a summary) offers a commitment to adopt 'all necessary measures for the speedy elimination of such intolerance in all its forms and manifestations and to prevent and combat discrimination on the ground of religion or belief'. The scale of ethnic violence, mass atrocity and genocide in the two decades following the 1981 Declaration on Religion and Belief is to some extent an indication of failure within the UN system and the global community. Yet such violence makes culturally related global commitments all the more necessary.

Box 8.2

Declaration on the Elimination of All Forms of Intolerance and of Discrimination Based on Religion or Belief
25 November 1981

Article 1 states that 'Everyone shall have the right to freedom of thought, conscience and religion. This right shall include freedom to have a religion or whatever belief of his choice, and freedom, either individually or in community with others and in public or private, to manifest his religion or belief in worship, observance, practice and teaching.' Further, no one shall be subject to coercion that would impair their freedom to have a religion or belief of their choice. Here, 'Freedom to manifest one's religion or belief may be subject only to such limitations as are prescribed by law and are necessary to protect public safety, order, health or morals or the fundamental rights and freedoms of others.'

Article 2 states that 'No one shall be subject to discrimination by any State, institution, group of persons, or person on the grounds of religion or other belief.' For the purposes of the Declaration, intolerance and discrimination based on religion or belief means 'any distinction, exclusion, restriction or preference based on religion or belief and having as its purpose or as its effect nullification or impairment of the recognition, enjoyment or exercise of human rights and fundamental freedoms on an equal basis'.

Article 3 states that 'Discrimination between human beings on the grounds of religion or belief constitutes an affront to human dignity and a disavowal of the principles of the Charter of the United Nations, and shall be condemned as a violation of the human rights and fundamental freedoms proclaimed in the Universal Declaration of Human Rights.' Such may be regarded as 'an obstacle to friendly and peaceful relations between nations'.

Article 4 sets forth the responsibilities of States to 'take effective measures to prevent and eliminate discrimination on the grounds of religion or belief in the recognition, exercise and enjoyment of human rights and fundamental freedoms in all fields of civil, economic, political, social and cultural life'.

Article 5 states that 'The parents or, as the case may be, the legal guardians of the child have the right to organize the life within the family in accordance with their religion or belief and bearing in mind the moral education in which they believe the child should be brought up.' Article 5 also contains reference to the rights of the child to have 'access to education in the matter of religion or belief' according to the wishes of parents or guardians.

Article 6 outlines in more detail what is meant by 'the right to freedom of thought, conscience, religion or belief', including the following freedoms:

'(a) To worship or assemble in connection with a religion or belief, and to establish and maintain places for these purposes;

(b) To establish and maintain appropriate charitable or humanitarian institutions;

(c) To make, acquire and use to an adequate extent the necessary articles and materials related to the rites or customs of a religion or belief;

continued

(d) To write, issue and disseminate relevant publications in these areas;
(e) To teach a religion or belief in places suitable for these purposes;
(f) To solicit and receive voluntary financial and other contributions from individuals and institutions;
(g) To train, appoint, elect or designate by succession appropriate leaders called for by the requirements and standards of any religion or belief;
(h) To observe days of rest and to celebrate holidays and ceremonies in accordance with the precepts of one's religion or belief;
(i) To establish and maintain communications with individuals and communities in matters of religion and belief at the national and international levels.'
Article 7 states that 'The rights and freedoms set forth in the present Declaration shall be accorded in national legislation in such a manner that everyone shall be able to avail himself of such rights and freedoms in practice.'
Article 8 states that 'Nothing in the present Declaration shall be construed as restricting or derogating from any right defined in the Universal Declaration of Human Rights and the International Covenants on Human Rights.'

For a full text, follow links at www.unhchr.org

After relatively low-level explicit treatment of religion, with the 1981 Declaration the UN system began to recognise the international significance of religion for a stable world order. Thus, during the 1990s, religion emerged in numerous international statements, gaining a new and unprecedented prominence (again, see Box 8.1). This included recognition by both the 1981 Declaration and the 1998 Oslo Declaration that freedom of religion extended to the more general *belief*, to allow for a wider interpretation of worldviews.

The World Conference Against Racism, Racial Discrimination, Xenophobia and Related Intolerance took place days before the attack on the Twin Towers in New York on 11 September 2001. While dealing with wider issues beyond religious freedom and belief, these remained integral to the Conference's concerns. The preamble to the Conference statement reaffirmed principles of non-discrimination:

> the principles of equality and non-discrimination in the Universal Declaration of Human Rights and encouraging respect for human rights and fundamental freedoms for all without distinction of any kind such as race, colour, sex, language, religion, political or other opinion, national or social origin, property, birth or other status.

If the events of 11 September 2001 brought religion – in all the claims and counter-claims about its role in international terrorism – into heightened focus, the US had for some years previous to this realised the importance of religion as a gauge of other marks of democratic citizenship:

A commitment to the inviolable and universal dignity of the human person is at the core of U.S. human rights policy abroad, including the policy of advocating religious freedom. Governments that protect religious freedom for all their citizens are more likely to protect the other fundamental human rights. Encouraging stable, healthy democracies is a vital national interest in the United States. The spread of democracy makes for good neighbours, economic prosperity, increased trade, and a decrease in conflict.

(US Department of State 2001)

The US Department of State makes claim to draw upon two sources here: 'the history and commitment of the American people, and standards established by the international community'. These two traditions are said to be not only 'consistent' but 'mutually supportive'.

Thus the 1998 International Religious Freedom Act made it a requirement for the US Secretary of State to publish an Annual Report on religious freedom worldwide to be submitted to the Committee on International Relations at the US House of Representatives and the Committee on Foreign Relations of the US Senate by the Department of State. The Report provides country-by-country accounts of religious freedoms and related democratic analyses. It is available at www.house.gov/international _relations/ and www.state.gov/g/drl/rls/irf/2001 (or whichever date the Report refers to). Coverage includes the following breakdown of regions:

* Africa
* East Asia and the Pacific
* Europe and Eurasia
* Near East and North Africa
* South Asia
* Western Hemisphere

The Report also contains an executive summary.

The introduction to the Report thus speaks of the longstanding commitment of the United States to religious liberty:

America's founders made religious freedom the first freedom of the Constitution – giving it pride of place among those liberties enumerated in the Bill of Rights – because they believed that guaranteeing the right to search for transcendent truths and ultimate human purpose was a critical component of a durable democracy.

(US Department of State 2001)

It goes on to reiterate how, in the international domain, 'Freedom of religion and conscience is one of the foundational rights in the post-War system of human rights instruments.' It again makes explicit how, in 'recent years, the international commitment to religious freedom has increased'.

NGOs are also increasingly interested in religious freedom as a measure of other basic citizenship rights. The world's foremost NGO concerned with such issues is Freedom House. One of its major publications is a global report on religious freedom (Marshall 2000), which usefully supplements the US Department of State Report on International Religious Freedom with independent commentary. Marshall's astute analysis recognises that 'surveying religious freedom is more limited than surveying human rights in general'. Marshall also links but differentiates freedom of religion and belief and freedom of expression, suggesting it is:

> different from surveying particular human rights, such as press freedom, which focus only on particular organizations or practices. With freedom of the press, one can look at the intensity of controls on particular media and the weight of penalties applied with those controls. But, unlike press freedom, religious freedom cannot be focused on the freedoms of certain organizations and individuals. Religious freedom cuts across a wide range of human rights.

Marshall uses the following criteria to define religious freedom:

> First, it refers to the freedoms of particular bodies, houses of worship, humanitarian organizations, educational institutions, and so forth. Second, it refers to freedom for particular individual religious practices – prayer, worship, dress, proclamation, diet, and so forth. Third, it refers to human rights in general in so far as they involve particular religious bodies, individuals, and activities. For example, the freedom to proclaim one's religion or belief is an issue of freedom of speech generally and is parallel to freedom of speech in other areas of life. Similarly, for freedom of the press or freedom of association. This means that we are looking not only at particular 'religious rights' but also at any human right, insofar as it impacts on freedom of religion or belief. In particular, we need to be aware of any different and unequal treatment of particular religions. This means that the question of adverse discrimination needs specific attention.

Some of Marshall's thought-provoking case studies are presented in Box 8.3.

Box 8.3

Guidance on defining abuses of religious freedom

- A European country bans Islamic dress in schools. This is a violation of religious freedom since, while the school may legitimately want to enforce a dress code, that should be outweighed by a right to live according to one's religion. If it were a case of a full covering and veil and the school were worried about checking someone's identity, say at exam time, then there might be additional legitimate concerns, but a way could be found around them.

continued

- A country bans polygamy or polyandry whereas some religions allow it. This is not a violation of religious freedom since no religion requires polygamy or polyandry.
- A country has a state church or its equivalent but otherwise allows freedom of religion. This is always an instance of religious discrimination and, therefore, a limit on religious freedom; however, its importance may vary greatly. Does the state fund the church in a way that it does not fund other religious bodies? Does the church have political privileges or privileges in areas such as education?
- A religious group is also a politically separatist group. . . . The question of whether the repression of such a group is a violation of religious freedom would depend on whether the group had a religious identity and on the justice of their cause. If there has been such a previous threat to the religious identity of the group, then the repression even of a separatist group would be a violation of religious freedom, and any human rights violations in the area are also violations of religious freedom. If a religiously identified separatist or other group is violent, the answer would depend on whether their violence is a legitimate form of self-defence or whether the group is inherently violent or terrorist. In the former case any human rights violations against them would also be violations of religious freedom.
- Are restrictions on the entrance of missionaries or other religious workers a violation of religious freedom? Not necessarily, as there is no universal right to be able to work in a country other than one's own. It would depend on whether such restrictions discriminated between (and within) religions and whether they had an adverse effect on domestic groups that are denied adequate, trained leadership.
- A decision by a country either to fund or not to fund education by religious groups can be consistent with religious freedom. The question is one of discrimination, that is, whether some groups are denied funds because of their beliefs while others are given funds.

(Marshall 2000: 14–16)

Many of these questions have an increasing relevance in a post-September 11 world.

Freedom of religion and belief through religious education: planning notes

Given the foregoing historical-legal-political grounding, what we need to do as religious educators is integrate the key aspects of freedom of religion and belief appropriate to a religious education context. This means identifying the explicit religious context and planning for explicitly religious education learning outcomes.

While presenting particular lesson plans might be prescriptive, what is offered here – adapting the structure of the QCA *Model Syllabuses for Religious Education* – is a suggested typology (Boxes 8.4.1 to 8.4.3), identifying:

- Attainment targets in religious education
- Skills and processes in religious education
- Attitudes in religious education

What follows (Box 8.4.4) is a series of suggested links for this theme to National Curriculum citizenship.

Box 8.4.1

Freedom of religion and belief: attainment targets in religious education

Attainment target 1: Learning about religions
Explore religious language, stories and symbolism that enable an individual or a people to challenge religious repression, and religious language, stories and symbolism that, by contrast, have allowed religious people to be instigators of religious repression.

Attainment target 2: Learning from religions
Give an informed and considered response to issues of freedom in religion and belief.

Box 8.4.2

Freedom of religion and belief: skills and processes in religious education

Investigation
Asking relevant questions about freedom of religion and belief.
Knowing how to access and use different types of sources as a way of gathering information about freedom of religion and belief – secular and religious, governmental and NGO.

Interpretation
The ability to draw from artefacts, works of art, poetry and symbolism concerning freedom of religion and belief.

Reflection
The ability to reflect on feelings, relationships, experience, ultimate questions, beliefs and practices in the face of religious persecution.

Empathy
The ability to consider the thoughts, feelings, experiences, attitudes, beliefs and values of others who suffer ridicule or even violent persecution for their beliefs.

Evaluation
The ability to debate issues around the justification for religious repression and persecution.

Analysis
Distinguishing between opinion, belief and fact, especially in assessments of propaganda,

continued

prejudice, and the extremes of discrimination, targeted at cultural, ethnic and religious minorities.

Synthesis
Linking significant features of political and religious ideologies together, understanding how differing viewpoints are held in tension in democratic plural societies.

Application
Making the association between religions and individual, community, national and international life, identifying key religious values and their interplay with secular ones, especially in the role of NGOs in the field of freedom of religion and belief.

Expression
The ability to explain the persistence of concepts, rituals and practices associated with religion in the face of historical and contemporary persecution.
The ability to identify and articulate matters of deep conviction and concern, and respond to religious questions through a variety of media – art, music, the novel.

Box 8.4.3
Freedom of religion and belief: attitudes in religious education

Commitment
Understanding the importance of commitment to a set of values by which to live one's life, often against all reason for hope.

Fairness
Considering other views carefully; a willingness to consider evidence and argument; the readiness to look beyond surface impressions to signs of hope and truth.

Respect
Recognising the need to respect those who have different beliefs and customs; recognising the rights of others to hold their own views; the avoidance of ridicule; and the discernment of what is worthy of respect and what is not.

Self-understanding
Developing a mature sense of self-worth and value, developing the capacity to discern the personal relevance of religious questions.

Enquiry
A desire to seek the truth, developing a personal interest in metaphysical questions, and the tension between mutually opposed and strongly held views.

Box 8.4.4

Freedom of religion and belief: National Curriculum citizenship links

Knowledge and understanding about becoming informed citizens
1   Pupils should be taught about:
a   the legal and human rights and responsibilities underpinning society and how they relate to citizens, including the role and operation of the criminal and civil justice systems
b   the origins and implications of the diverse national, regional, religious and ethnic identities in the United Kingdom and the need for mutual respect and understanding
POSSIBLE RELIGIOUS EDUCATION LINK: attitudes to religious freedom in religious communities in the United Kingdom.

Developing skills of enquiry and communication
2   Pupils should be taught to:
a   research a topical political, spiritual, moral, social or cultural issue, problem or event by analysing information from different sources, including ICT-based sources, showing an awareness of the use and abuse of statistics
b   express, justify and defend orally and in writing a personal opinion about such issues, problems or events
c   contribute to group and exploratory class discussions, and take part in formal debates
POSSIBLE RELIGIOUS EDUCATION LINKS: See Question, discuss, research activities in Box 8.5.

Developing skills of participation and responsible action
3   Pupils should be taught to:
a   use their imagination to consider other people's experiences and be able to think about, express, explain and critically evaluate views that are not their own
b   negotiate, decide and take part responsibly in school- and community-based activities
c   reflect on the process of participating
POSSIBLE RELIGIOUS EDUCATION LINKS: See Question, discuss, research activities in Box 8.5.

Conclusion

Like freedom of expression, freedom of religion and belief is often an indicator of a country's wider treatment of its citizenship. Freedom of religion and belief is therefore of critical concern for all, but religious educators must have, for obvious reasons, a special interest. With Box 8.5 presenting a range of related issues, this interest becomes a delicate matter when it is religious traditions themselves that are restricting the religious freedoms of others.

Box 8.5

Freedom of religion and belief through religious education: question, discuss, research

Question and discuss

1   Many of the world's major religious texts (the Bible, the Qur'an) have been banned – why?
2   Freedom of religion and belief is a fundamental cultural freedom as well as a basic civil and political right. Why are religions some of the worst offenders against the cultural and religious freedoms of others?
3   Religious intolerance remains one of the most frequent causes of war – why?
4   In what ways is being religious more dangerous today than it ever has been? Or are there periods in recent or distant history when it was more so (Stalinist Russia, for instance, or the China of Mao and the Cultural Revolution)?
5   If the UN takes religious freedom seriously, why has it taken it so long (until the early 1990s) to make a specific declaration about the rights of religious believers?
6   What if anything do you think might have motivated a relative silence about religion at the UN since its creation in 1945?
7   The US State Department's Annual Report on Religious Freedom – required by law since 1998 – represents a substantial investment of US tax-payers' money. What do you think motivates the US interest in religion, given that in its own Constitution the US government may not interfere with matters of religion by law?

Research

8   Visit the Freedom House website at www.freedomhouse.org. Find one instance of the repression of religious freedom by a State or by a political ideology (such as communism) aligned to a State. Now find one instance of the repression of religious freedom *in the name of religion*.
9   Visit the website for the World Conference Against Racism, Xenophobia and Other Forms of Discrimination, held in Durban, South Africa (September 2001), at www.un.org/wcar
10 Visit the Human Rights Watch website. Follow the global links to the following: China/Tibet; India; Israel; Georgia; Sudan. In view of Marshall's (2000) guidance, what are key human rights issues of religious freedom in each of these complex political situations, and how far are religious factors a part of, integral to, or nothing to do with the political situation?

Chapter 9

Economic rights, environmental responsibilities

Sustainable development through religious education

Introduction

Hunger, starvation and the extremes of deprivation – as well as the relative forms of these – present massive ethical issues for all and not just religious educators. Many NGOs are religious-based and together with secular and governmental agencies work tirelessly to achieve a world in which such living horrors do not exist. Such basic human rights are about meeting the most fundamental human needs. But the right to development, as we shall see, extends beyond the 'mere' right to survival, into areas familiar to educators in the United Kingdom – covering social and cultural, moral and spiritual development as well as more physical needs. With increasing world population, however, the right to development, for individuals and peoples, often clashes – both in rich, developed countries of the northern hemisphere and in poorer, developing countries in the southern hemisphere – with other issues, notably those of environmental protection, the protection of biodiversity and sustainable development. All provide important educational material for the religious educator wanting to make a genuine contribution to citizenship.

Economic rights, environmental responsibilities: historical-legal-political background

The preamble to the Declaration on the Right to Development highlights the notion of the indivisibility of all rights. It recognises that:

> development is a comprehensive economic, social, cultural and political process, which aims at the constant improvement of the well-being of the entire population and of all individuals on the basis of their active, free and meaningful participation in development and in the fair distribution of benefits resulting therefrom.

Indeed, it recalls the provisions of both the International Covenant on Economic, Social and Cultural Rights and the International Covenant on Civil and Political Rights, and in so doing, 'the right of peoples to self-determination, by virtue of which they have the right freely to determine their political status and to pursue their economic, social and cultural development'. It also recognises 'the right of peoples to exercise, subject to the relevant provisions of both International Covenants on Human Rights, full and complete sovereignty over all their natural wealth and resources'. What would have been unthinkable in 1948, and increasingly inevitable in 1966, was the sense of historical injustice done by the presently wealthy and former colonial powers so instrumental in drawing up the Universal Declaration of Human Rights. Boxes 9.1 and 9.2 present historic landmarks in the international recognition of the right to development as a fundamental human right. Yet big earth summits have also been criticised for achieving little in practice. Rio + 10, the world summit on sustainable development, was amongst those so criticised. The preparatory meeting, before this particular event got under way, was held in the luxurious resort setting of Bali, and many regarded the opulent setting as insensitive when issues like global poverty were under discussion. (The bombing of otherwise peaceful Bali only months later was an atrocity that shocked the world.) More general protests by 'anti-globalisation' alliances often receive high-profile news coverage when they occur.

Box 9.1

Human rights and development: historical landmarks

World Conference on Human Rights (Vienna, 1993)
Vienna + 5

International Conference on Population and Development (Cairo, 1994)
Cairo + 5

World Summit for Social Development (Copenhagen, 1995)
Copenhagen + 5

Fourth World Conference on Women (Beijing, 1995)
Beijing + 5

World Conference Against Racism, Racial Discrimination, Xenophobia and Related Intolerance (Durban, 2001)

Rio + 10: World Summit on Sustainable Development (Johannesburg, 2–11 September 2002)

Working Group on the Right to Development (7–18 October 2002)

For full texts of the relevant documents, follow links at www.undp.org

---

Box 9.2

International legal standards: defending the right to development

Universal Declaration on the Eradication of Hunger and Malnutrition (16 November 1964)
Declaration on Social Progress and Development (11 December 1969)
Declaration on the Rights of Mentally Retarded Persons (20 December 1971)
Declaration on the Use of Scientific and Technological Progress in the Interests of Peace and for the Benefit of Mankind (10 November 1975)
Declaration on the Rights of Disabled Persons (9 December 1975)
Declaration on the Right of Peoples to Peace (12 November 1984)
Declaration on the Right to Development (4 December 1986)
Guidelines for the Regulation of Computerized Personal Data Files (14 December 1990)
International Convention on the Protection of the Rights of All Migrant Workers and Members of Their Families (18 December 1990)
Principles for the protection of persons with mental illness and the improvement of mental health care (17 December 1991)
Universal Declaration on the Human Genome and Human Rights (UNESCO) (c. 2001)

Right to enjoy culture, international cultural development and co-operation
Declaration of the Principles of International Cultural Co-operation (UNESCO) (4 November 1966)
Recommendation concerning Education for International Understanding, Co-operation and Peace and Education relating to Human Rights and Fundamental Freedoms (UNESCO) (19 November 1974)

For full texts, follow links at www.unhchr.org

The Declaration on the Right to Development, adopted by the UN General Assembly on 4 December 1986, sets the issue of development in historical and especially colonial and postcolonial context. While responsibility for present economic inequalities cannot all be placed at the foot of past empires or indeed present multinationals, the UN recognised that 'massive and flagrant violations of the human rights of the peoples and individuals' affected by 'colonialism, neo-colonialism, apartheid, all forms of racism and racial discrimination, foreign domination and occupation' have contributed to poverty and underdevelopment in many countries. In addition, the elimination of 'aggression and threats against national sovereignty, national unity and territorial integrity and threats of war' would contribute to 'circumstances propitious to the development of a great part of mankind'. In other words, the UN makes a clear link between war and civil disturbance and underdevelopment. There was thus reiteration that 'international peace and security are essential elements for the realization of the right to development', and 'that there is a close relationship between disarmament and development' and 'that resources released through disarmament measures should be devoted to the economic and social development and well-being of all peoples and, in particular, those of the developing countries'. Box 9.3 presents many of the largely unfulfilled aspirations of the international community.

Box 9.3

Declaration on the Right to Development
Adopted by the UN General Assembly, 4 December 1986

Article 1 states that the right to development is 'an inalienable human right by virtue of which every human person and all peoples are entitled to participate in, contribute to, and enjoy economic, social, cultural and political development, in which all human rights and fundamental freedoms can be fully realized'. According to the Declaration this implies 'the full realization of the right of peoples to self-determination, which includes . . . the exercise of their inalienable right to full sovereignty over all their natural wealth and resources'.

Article 2 states that 'the human person is the central subject of development and should be the active participant and beneficiary of the right to development'. Article 2 also speaks of the responsibility of all human beings for development, 'individually and collectively', and 'duties to the community' as well as rights and freedoms. It also reiterates the responsibilities of States 'to formulate appropriate national development policies that aim at the constant improvement of the well-being of the entire population and of all individuals, on the basis of their active, free and meaningful participation in development and in the fair distribution of the benefits resulting therefrom'.

Article 3 sets forth the 'primary responsibility' of States to provide 'for the creation of national and international conditions favourable to the realization of the right to development'. States also have 'the duty to co-operate with each other in ensuring development and eliminating obstacles to development. States should realize their rights and fulfil their duties in such a manner as to promote a new international economic order based on sovereign equality, interdependence, mutual interest and co-operation among all States, as well as to encourage the observance and realization of human rights.'

Article 4 sets forth the responsibility of States 'to take steps, individually and collectively, to formulate international development policies with a view to facilitating the full realization of the right to development'.

Article 5 sets forth the responsibility of States to 'take resolute steps to eliminate the massive and flagrant violations of the human rights of peoples and human beings affected by situations such as those resulting from apartheid, all forms of racism and racial discrimination, colonialism, foreign domination and occupation, aggression, foreign interference and threats against national sovereignty, national unity and territorial integrity, threats of war and refusal to recognize the fundamental right of peoples to self-determination'.

Article 6 elaborates the principle that 'All States should co-operate with a view to promoting, encouraging and strengthening universal respect for and observance of all human rights and fundamental freedoms for all without any distinction as to race, sex, language or

continued

religion.' It also emphasises that 'All human rights and fundamental freedoms are indivisible and interdependent; equal attention and urgent consideration should be given to the implementation, promotion and protection of civil, political, economic, social and cultural rights.'

Article 7 sets forth the principle that 'All States should promote the establishment, maintenance and strengthening of international peace and security and, to that end, should do their utmost to achieve general and complete disarmament under effective international control, as well as to ensure that the resources released by effective disarmament measures are used for comprehensive development, in particular that of the developing countries.'

Article 8 sets forth the principle that 'States should undertake, at the national level, all necessary measures for the realization of the right to development and shall ensure, inter alia, equality of opportunity for all in their access to basic resources, education, health services, food, housing, employment and the fair distribution of income.'

Article 9 reiterates the principle of the 'indivisible and interdependent' nature of the rights set forth in the Declaration that 'each of them should be considered in the context of the whole'.

Article 10 sets forth the principle that 'Steps should be taken to ensure the full exercise and progressive enhancement of the right to development, including the formulation, adoption and implementation of policy, legislative and other measures at the national and international levels.'

For the full text, follow links at www.unhchr.org

UNDP is the UN's global development network 'advocating for change and connecting countries to knowledge, experience and resources to help people build a better life'. UNDP works on the ground in over 160 countries. Its various networks assist national governments to achieve the Millennium Development Goals (MDGs), including the halving of world poverty by 2015. The UNDP identifies a number of areas of strategic operation called 'Thematic Trust Funds', towards which finance and other support is directed. The Thematic Trust Funds are:

- Democratic Governance, including Project Summaries
- Poverty Reduction
- Energy
- Environment
- Information and Communications Technology
- HIV/AIDS
- Gender

These are designed as 'results-oriented programmes at the country, regional and global levels'. Across all these activities, UNDP is committed to 'the protection of human rights and the empowerment of women'. Again, we see the theory and practice of sustainable development suffused and being underpinned by the language of human rights. Box 9.4 summarises the role of the UNDP at the World Summit on Sustainable Development in its promotion of 'Capacity 2015'.

Box 9.4
UNDP and Capacity 2015

UNDP IS SEEKING GLOBAL ENDORSEMENT AND SUPPORT FOR THE CAPACITY 2015 PLATFORM. Capacity 2015's overall goal is to develop the capacities needed by developing countries and countries in transition to meet their sustainable development goals under Agenda 21 and the Millennium Development Goals. It will orient and support a number of key capacity development initiatives, including developing capacities for local sustainable development, national sustainable development strategies, local capacity development for Multilateral Environmental Agreements, developing capacities to reduce vulnerability in small island developing states (SIDS) and a strategic capacity development facility. Capacity 2015, operating globally and nationally, will help developing and transition countries ensure co-ordination, mutual support and maximum synergies among partners' capacity development efforts.

The Capacity 2015 approach involves:
* Addressing local capacity development needs, tying them to national economic, social and environmental policy and processes.
* Helping local groups, and their supporting local and national governments, private sectors and civil society organisations to overcome capacity constraints to achieving economic, social and environmental sustainability.
* Promoting local, national, regional and global partnerships among public and private sectors and the major groups of civil society, giving each new opportunities to bring to bear on their respective strengths and resources and learn from one another.
* Ensuring strong synergies among all relevant capacity development initiatives, particularly those related to multilateral environmental treaties, poverty reduction strategies and sustainable development strategies.

Expected outcomes of Capacity 2015 include the following:
* Developing countries and countries in transition accelerate their implementation of Agenda 21 and their achievement of the Millennium Development Goals.
* National and local policies and legislation reviewed and revised, eliminating bottlenecks and ensuring strong and consistent incentives for local sustainable development.
* Local and national capacities (human, institutional and societal) developed and contributing to sustainable development, including poverty alleviation, in their communities.
* Networks formed, supporting civic engagement and responsible local leadership. Information and communications systems in place, helping communities participate in decisions governing their involvement in the global economy.
* Broad participatory platforms established, designing, implementing and monitoring strategies, plans and other planning instruments.

continued

> • Resource mobilisation campaigns activated, assisting communities to overcome marginalisation and other barriers to competing successfully in a globalising world.
> • Functional partnerships and networks involving communities with national, regional and international partners created, supporting local capacity development for sustainable development that includes poverty reduction.
>
> Further details at www.undp.org

Economic rights, environmental responsibilities through religious education: planning notes

Major development agencies such as Oxfam are not only seeing an integrated approach to sustainable economic development with social justice but are taking a rights-based approach to encompass all of their development work. For example, Oxfam believe that 'poverty is a state of powerlessness in which people are unable to exercise their basic rights', and work on the principle that 'all people enjoy certain rights' and that this 'provides not only a moral basis for our work, but also a legal one' because 'rights are enshrined in international agreements, covenants and declarations signed on to by the great majority of the world's governments at international summits and conferences'. The rights approach of Oxfam includes the following:

- The right to a sustainable livelihood – basic needs such as food, shelter and clean water should be achievable for all; people should be able to preserve the natural resources on which they depend.
- The right to services – health, education and other services should be available to all.
- The right to life and security – people should live free from fear or displacement due to wars, crime and other violence.
- The right to be heard – people should be able to organise, speak out and take part in decisions which affect them.
- The right to an identity – people should live free from discrimination on the grounds of gender, ethnicity or other issues of identity.

(For further details, visit www.oxfam.org.uk)

When working on issues of economic rights, responsibilities and sustainable development, it will be interesting for religious educators to compare these aims of an avowedly secular NGO working in development with those of religiously-based NGOs.

In planning for citizenship through religious education, it is thus crucial that neither the explicit religious education nor conscious citizenship elements of delivery are lost, but in the range of available resources, religious educators can find much of direct relevance – see Box 9.5.

Box 9.5

The right to development: learning resource links

United Nations Development Programme (UNDP) – New York, USA
www.undp.org

Global Compact
(www.unglobalcompact.org)

UN Human Development Report 2000: Human Rights and Human Development
www.undp.org/hdro/HDR2000

Civil Society Organizations and Participation Programme (CSOPP)
www.undp.org/csopp/CSO/index

Democratic Governance
www.magnet.undp.org

Indigenous peoples
www.undp.org/csopp/CSO/NewFiles/ipindex

World Bank Group – Washington, USA
www.worldbank.org

Human rights and development
www.worldbank.org/html/extdr/rights

The economics of civil wars, crime and violence
www.worldbank.org/research/conflict/index

World Food Programme (WFP) – Rome, Italy
www.wfp.org

United Nations University/World Institute for Development Economics Research
(UNU/WIDER)
www.wider.unu.edu

World Health Organization (WHO) – Geneva, Switzerland
www.who.int/home-page

Emergency and humanitarian action
www.who.int/eha/disasters

Health as a bridge for peace
www.who.int/eha/trares/hbp/index

Health as a human right
www.who.int/archives/who50/en/human

Given the foregoing historical-legal-political grounding, what we need to do as religious educators is integrate the key aspects of economic rights and environmental responsibilities appropriate to a religious education context. This means identifying the explicit religious context and planning for explicitly religious education learning outcomes.

While presenting particular lesson plans might be prescriptive, what is offered here – adapting the structure of the QCA *Model Syllabuses for Religious Education* – is a suggested typology (Boxes 9.6.1 to 9.6.3), identifying:

- Attainment targets in religious education
- Skills and processes in religious education
- Attitudes in religious education

What follows (Box 9.6.4) is a series of suggested links for this theme to National Curriculum citizenship.

Box 9.6.1

Economic rights, environmental responsibilities: attainment targets in religious education

Attainment target 1: Learning about religions
Identify key issues in the relationship between economic rights and environmental responsibilities.

Attainment target 2: Learning from religions
Give an informed and considered response to the religious and moral issues surrounding the tension between economic rights and environmental responsibilities.

Box 9.6.2

Economic rights, environmental responsibilities: skills and processes in religious education

Investigation
Asking relevant questions about economic rights and environmental responsibilities.

Interpretation
The ability to interpret the meaning of religious texts in the face of economic need and the potential conflict between meeting these economic needs and stewardship of the planet.

continued

Reflection
The ability to reflect on feelings, relationships, experience, ultimate questions, beliefs and practices in the face of human deprivation and environmental degradation.

Empathy
The ability to consider the thoughts, feelings, experiences, attitudes, beliefs and values of others in the face of human deprivation and environmental degradation.

Evaluation
The ability to debate issues of religious significance in the face of human deprivation and environmental degradation with reference to evidence and argument.

Analysis
Distinguishing between opinion, belief and fact in assessments of human need and environmental protection.

Synthesis
Linking significant features of religion together in relation to this fundamental conflict between human rights and environmental concern over the domination of human beings, especially theological views about the preordained superiority of humanity as the crown of creation.

Application
Making the association between religions and individual, community, national and international life, identifying key religious values and their interplay with secular ones, especially in the role of NGOs working in sustainable development.

Expression
The ability to identify and articulate matters of deep conviction and concern, and respond to basic human need and environmental concern, especially in time of mutual crisis, through a variety of media – art, music, the novel.

Box 9.6.3
Economic rights, environmental responsibilities: attitudes in religious education

Commitment
Understanding the importance of commitment to a set of values by which to live one's life, often against all reason for hope.

Fairness
Considering other views carefully; a willingness to consider evidence and argument; and the

continued

readiness to look for solutions to tensions between human rights and environmental concern.

Respect
Balancing the respect for human beings and their rights with the responsibilities of human beings to respect their environment for present and future generations.

Self-understanding
Developing a mature sense of self-worth and value, developing the capacity to discern the personal relevance of religious questions in relation to human rights and environmental issues.

Enquiry
A desire to seek practical solutions as well as conceptual resolutions to tensions between rights and responsibilities.

Box 9.6.4

Economic rights, environmental responsibilities: National Curriculum citizenship links

Knowledge and understanding about becoming informed citizens
1   Pupils should be taught about:
a   the legal and human rights and responsibilities underpinning society and how they relate to citizens, including the role and operation of the criminal and civil justice systems
POSSIBLE RELIGIOUS EDUCATION LINKS: Religion and the right to life.
e   how the economy functions, including the role of business and financial services
f   the opportunities for individuals and voluntary groups to bring about social change locally, nationally, in Europe and internationally
h   the rights and responsibilities of consumers, employers and employees
j   the wider issues and challenges of global interdependence and responsibility, including sustainable development and Local Agenda 21
POSSIBLE RELIGIOUS EDUCATION LINKS: The work of religiously-based NGOs.

Developing skills of enquiry and communication
2   Pupils should be taught to:
a   research a topical political, spiritual, moral, social or cultural issue, problem or event by analysing information from different sources, including ICT-based sources, showing an awareness of the use and abuse of statistics
b   express, justify and defend orally and in writing a personal opinion about such issues, problems or events
c   contribute to group and exploratory class discussions, and take part in formal debates
POSSIBLE RELIGIOUS EDUCATION LINKS: See Question, discuss, research activities in Box 9.7.

continued

Developing skills of participation and responsible action

3   Pupils should be taught to:
a   use their imagination to consider other people's experiences and be able to think about, express, explain and critically evaluate views that are not their own
b   negotiate, decide and take part responsibly in school- and community-based activities
c   reflect on the process of participating.
POSSIBLE RELIGIOUS EDUCATION LINKS: See Question, discuss, research activities in Box 9.7.

Conclusion

This chapter opened with the assertion that hunger, starvation and the extremes of deprivation present massive ethical issues for all and not just religious educators. Development, including both short-term humanitarian relief and longer-term development work, is one of the major areas in political life where religions gain credit from the widest possible public, including those normally sceptical of religious practice. Box 9.7 provides some points for developing and enhancing this positive view of religion through citizenship.

Box 9.7

Economic rights, environmental responsibilities through religious education: question, discuss, research

Question and discuss

1   Is there a reasonable answer from any religious tradition today as to why there are people hungry in a world where there is enough food to feed all?
2   The QCA model syllabuses and the majority of locally agreed syllabuses, along with most secondary examination boards at GCSE level, all feature the environment as a theme. All the major world faiths arose from a pre-modern, pre-industrialised landscape – to what extent are their claims to environmental consciousness a belated attempt to conceal fundamental failings in their records of stewardship of the earth?
3   Does the emphasis on human rights, and especially the right to development, betray a fundamental selfishness on behalf of human beings?
4   To what extent has religious 'otherworldliness' led to a neglect of the environment of planet Earth?
5   Do religious traditions today maintain poverty as a virtue? (Many religious orders still profess poverty within Christianity as a lifelong pledge.) To what extent is this different from the involuntary poverty of so much of the world's population?
6   Read the Sermon on the Mount in Matthew 5–7. Note and record all the references Jesus makes to money, wealth, poverty and attachment to worldly goods.

continued

To what extent was Jesus a good economist, or a naïve idealist, irresponsible when it came to matters of money and basic survival? Are these sorts of priorities right for the world today?

7 When asked about the payment of taxation to Caesar, Jesus said, 'Give to Caesar what is Caesar's and to God what is God's.' Evaluate this view of religion and state in today's Britain.

Research

8 Visit the Oxfam website. You will notice that Oxfam has adopted a 'rights approach' to development. Now visit the Cafod and Christian Aid websites. How do the rationales of the latter differ? To what extent is religion a factor in determining the mission of both Cafod and Christian Aid? What of, say, Jewish Aid, World Jewish Relief or Muslim Aid? What does this tell us about contemporary moral thinking about rights and responsibilities if religious and secular organisations can share ideals and action to eradicate suffering and poverty in the world?

9 Compare the religious ideals of the latter two, Christian-based organisations with the stated aims of Muslim Aid and/or Jewish Aid.

10 Visit the website of PAX Christi, a Christian organisation concerned with promoting peace and justice. To what extent is the arms race, or at least the civil defence budgets of developing countries, responsible for their poverty?

Chapter 10

Women's rights through religious education

Introduction

Religious traditions are quick to defend their credentials on a range of controversial issues. The rights of women, by contemporary secular standards, have not had a good track record within many religious traditions (Howland 1999). All sorts of arguments are advanced – including 'equal but different', historical context and cultural tradition. The matter has been largely neglected in religious education in favour of accommodating the most positive view of women in religious traditions according to the traditions themselves. This chapter highlights some of the key international legal and related standards on women's rights and presents a few outline suggestions about how this critical area of citizenship can be approached in religious education.

Women's rights: historical-legal-political background

Article 2 of the Universal Declaration of Human Rights underpins the notion that equality of rights in terms of gender is central to human rights in general: 'Everyone is entitled to all the rights and freedoms set forth in this Declaration, without distinction of any kind, such as race, colour, sex, language, religion, political or other opinion, national or social origin, property, birth or other status.' Women's rights and citizenship are integral; one can hardly be separated from the other (Jeffries 1999). Yet numerous studies show that the human rights of women are amongst the least respected in practice (UNICEF 1999; UN 2000; Rendel 1997; Askin and Koenig 2000; McColgan 2000; Agosin 2001; Beigbeder 2001; Schechter 2001).

Considerable efforts have been made since the 1948 Declaration to establish international legal standards for women's rights (UN 2002c, 2002g; UNICEF 1999), and a selection is presented in Box 10.1.

Foundational amongst these is the Convention on the Elimination of All Forms of Discrimination against Women, key passages of which are featured in Box 10.2.

One of the most high-profile international meetings to discuss women's rights as late twentieth- and early twenty-first-century citizens was the fourth World Conference on Women held in Beijing in 1995. The Beijing Declaration sets the context, tone and agenda for women's rights.

Box 10.1

International legal standards: defending women's rights

Convention on the Political Rights of Women (20 December 1952, into effect 7 July 1957)
Declaration on the Protection of Women and Children in Emergency and Armed Conflict
(14 December 1974)
Declaration on the Elimination of All Forms of Discrimination against Women (7 November
1967, into effect 3 September 1981)
Convention on the Elimination of All Forms of Discrimination against Women
(20 November 1989)
Declaration on the Elimination of Violence against Women (20 December 1993)
Optional Protocol to the Convention on the Elimination of Discrimination against Women
(10 December 1999, into effect 22 December 2000)

For full texts of the documents, follow links at www.unhchr.ch/html/menu3

Box 10.2

Convention on the Elimination of All Forms of Discrimination Against Women
Adopted 18 December 1979, entry into force 3 September 1981

PART I
Article I defines 'discrimination against women' as meaning 'any distinction, exclusion or restriction made on the basis of sex which has the effect or purpose of impairing or nullifying the recognition, enjoyment or exercise by women, irrespective of their marital status, on a basis of equality of men and women, of human rights and fundamental freedoms in the political, economic, social, cultural, civil or any other field'.
Article 2 commits States to condemn 'discrimination against women in all its forms, agree to pursue by all appropriate means and without delay a policy of eliminating discrimination against women and, to this end, undertake:
(a) To embody the principle of the equality of men and women in their national constitutions or other appropriate legislation if not yet incorporated therein and to ensure, through law and other appropriate means, the practical realization of this principle;
(b) To adopt appropriate legislative and other measures, including sanctions where appropriate, prohibiting all discrimination against women;
(c) To establish legal protection of the rights of women on an equal basis with men and to ensure through competent national tribunals and other public institutions the effective protection of women against any act of discrimination;
(d) To refrain from engaging in any act or practice of discrimination against women and to ensure that public authorities and institutions shall act in conformity with this obligation;

continued

(e) To take all appropriate measures to eliminate discrimination against women by any person, organization or enterprise;

(f) To take all appropriate measures, including legislation, to modify or abolish existing laws, regulations, customs and practices which constitute discrimination against women;

(g) To repeal all national penal provisions which constitute discrimination against women.'

Article 3 commits States to 'take in all fields, in particular in the political, social, economic and cultural fields, all appropriate measures, including legislation, to ensure the full development and advancement of women, for the purpose of guaranteeing them the exercise and enjoyment of human rights and fundamental freedoms on a basis of equality with men'.

Article 4 states that special measures aimed at 'accelerating de facto equality between men and women shall not be considered discrimination as defined in the present Convention, but shall in no way entail as a consequence the maintenance of unequal or separate standards; these measures shall be discontinued when the objectives of equality of opportunity and treatment have been achieved'. It also states that special measures 'aimed at protecting maternity shall not be considered discriminatory'.

Article 5 commits States to take appropriate measures:

(a) 'To modify the social and cultural patterns of conduct of men and women, with a view to achieving the elimination of prejudices and customary and all other practices which are based on the idea of the inferiority or the superiority of either of the sexes or on stereotyped roles for men and women;

(b) To ensure that family education includes a proper understanding of maternity as a social function and the recognition of the common responsibility of men and women in the upbringing and development of their children, it being understood that the interest of the children is the primordial consideration in all cases.'

Article 6 commits States to 'take all appropriate measures, including legislation, to suppress all forms of traffic in women and exploitation of prostitution of women'.

PART II

Article 7 commits States to 'take all appropriate measures to eliminate discrimination against women in the political and public life of the country', particularly the right to vote, to be eligible for election, to hold public office and participate in government.

Article 8 commits States to 'take all appropriate measures to ensure to women, on equal terms with men and without any discrimination, the opportunity to represent their Governments at the international level and to participate in the work of international organizations'.

Article 9 commits States to 'grant women equal rights with men to acquire, change or retain their nationality. They shall ensure in particular that neither marriage to an alien nor change of nationality by the husband during marriage shall automatically change the nationality of the wife, render her stateless or force upon her the nationality of the husband.' It also commits States to 'grant women equal rights with men with respect to the nationality of their children'.

continued

PART III
Article 10 commits States to ensuring equal rights in education, including career and vocational guidance. This article includes detailed reference to a wide range of measures such as access to the same curricula and examinations. There is a commitment to 'the elimination of any stereotyped concept of the roles of men and women at all levels'. Coeducation is to be encouraged, as too 'the revision of textbooks and school programmes and the adaptation of teaching methods'.
Article 11 commits States 'to eliminate discrimination against women in the field of employment'. This detailed article contains reference to work as an 'inalienable right', equality of opportunity of employment at all stages from application onwards, and particular rights and protections of women in regard to maternity.
Article 12 commits States to 'take all appropriate measures to eliminate discrimination against women in the field of health care in order to ensure, on a basis of equality of men and women, access to health care services, including those related to family planning'.
Article 13 commits States to 'take all appropriate measures to eliminate discrimination against women in other areas of economic and social life in order to ensure, on a basis of equality of men and women, the same rights, in particular:
(a) The right to family benefits;
(b) The right to bank loans, mortgages and other forms of financial credit;
(c) The right to participate in recreational activities, sports and all aspects of cultural life.'
Article 14 commits States to 'take into account the particular problems faced by rural women and the significant roles which rural women play in the economic survival of their families'.

PART IV
Article 15 commits States to 'accord to women equality with men before the law'.
Article 16 commits States to 'take all appropriate measures to eliminate discrimination against women in all matters relating to marriage and family relations', including consent to marry and the 'same rights and responsibilities during marriage and at its dissolution'.

For a full text of the document, follow links at www.unhchr.org

The Conference:

Determined to advance the goals of equality, development and peace for all women everywhere in the interest of all humanity,
Acknowledging the voices of all women everywhere and taking note of the diversity of women and their roles and circumstances, honouring the women who paved the way and inspired by the hope present in the world's youth,
Recognize that the status of women has advanced in some important respects in the past decade but that progress has been uneven, inequalities between women and men have persisted and major obstacles remain, with serious consequences for the well-being of all people,

Also recognize that this situation is exacerbated by the increasing poverty that is affecting the lives of the majority of the world's people, in particular women and children, with origins in both the national and international domains,
Dedicate ourselves unreservedly to addressing these constraints and obstacles and thus enhancing further the advancement and empowerment of women all over the world, and agree that this requires urgent action in the spirit of determination, hope, co-operation and solidarity, now and to carry us forward into the next century.

The Conference was also convinced that 'Women's empowerment and their full participation on the basis of equality in all spheres of society, including participation in the decision-making process and access to power, are fundamental for the achievement of equality, development and peace'. Commitments made by the Beijing Declaration included:

- Full implementation of the human rights of women and of the girl child 'as an inalienable, integral and indivisible part of all human rights and fundamental freedoms'.
- The empowerment and advancement of women 'including the right to freedom of thought, conscience, religion and belief'.

Broken down, these included a determination to:

- Take effective action against violations of women's basic rights and freedoms
- Eliminate all forms of discrimination against women and the girl child
- Remove all obstacles to gender equality and the empowerment of women
- Encourage participation of men in the development of gender equality
- Promote women's economic independence
- Eradicate the persistent and increasing burden of poverty on women
- Promote people-centred sustainable development, especially by the provision of basic and lifelong education for girls and women
- Ensure peace for the advancement of women
- Prevent and eliminate all forms of violence against women and girls
- Ensure equal access to and equal treatment of women in education
- Ensure equal access to and equal treatment of women in health care
- Overcome barriers to women's empowerment through factors such as race, age, language, ethnicity, culture, religion, disability or indigenous identity
- Ensure respect for international law, including humanitarian law, in order to protect women and girls in particular

'Beijing+5 Process and Beyond' was a focus for the twenty-third special session of the General Assembly on 'Women 2000: Gender Equality, Development and Peace for the Twenty-first Century' held at UN Headquarters in New York from 5 June to 9 June 2000. The conference outcomes were framed in a document entitled 'Further Actions and Initiatives to Implement the Beijing Declaration and Platform for Action'.

Box 10.3

Women's rights: UN links

United Nations Development Fund for Women (UNIFEM) – New York, USA
www.unifem.undp.org

Integrating Gender into the Third World Conference against Racism, Racial Discrimination, Xenophobia and Related Intolerance
www.unifem.undp.org/hr_racism

WomenWatch – New York, USA
www.un.org/womenwatch

Division for the Advancement of Women
www.un.org/womenwatch/daw

Documents and databases
www.un.org/womenwatch/resources

The UN working for women
www.un.org/womenwatch/un

UN conferences and events
www.un.org/womenwatch/confer

Women's rights through religious education: planning notes

Given the foregoing historical-legal-political grounding, what we need to do as religious educators is integrate the key aspects of women's rights appropriate to a religious education context. This means identifying the explicit religious context and planning for explicitly religious education learning outcomes.

While presenting particular lesson plans might be prescriptive, what is offered here – adapting the structure of the QCA *Model Syllabuses for Religious Education* – is a suggested typology (Boxes 10.4.1 to 10.4.3), identifying:

- Attainment targets in religious education
- Skills and processes in religious education
- Attitudes in religious education

What follows (Box 10.4.4) is a series of suggested links for this theme to National Curriculum citizenship.

Box 10.4.1

Women's rights: attainment targets in religious education

Attainment target 1: Learning about religions

Identify and explore critical issues for theology and gender.

Identify and explore issues centred around women's rights that have a bearing upon religious traditions in the world today, possibly linking in with the worst abuses, including genocide and ethnic cleansing in Europe – in the former Yugoslavia – especially gender- and religious-focused violence against minorities.

Attainment target 2: Learning from religions

Give an informed and considered response to the religious and moral issues in relation to theology and gender in social, political and economic context.

Identify and respond to questions of meaning which gender-based violence and other abuses of human rights against women raise for our own lives and our own treatment of people.

Box 10.4.2

Women's rights: skills and processes in religious education

Investigation

Asking relevant theological questions about women's rights.

Knowing how to use different types of sources as a way of gathering information about women's rights from a variety of secular and traditional sources.

Interpretation

The ability to draw from artefacts, works of art, poetry and symbolism reflecting the role of women in religion and society, and the ability to suggest the meaning of religious texts that present the variety of shades of interpretation.

Reflection

The ability to reflect on feelings, relationships, experience, ultimate questions, beliefs and practices in the face of the prejudice and discrimination suffered by women and girls.

Empathy

The ability to consider in a balanced and insightful way women's perception of the issues about their roles in social and cultural, political and economic as well as religious life.

continued

Evaluation
The ability to debate issues of religious significance with reference to evidence and argument in relation to women's role in social and cultural, political and economic as well as religious life.

Analysis
Distinguishing between opinion, belief and fact, especially in assessments of propaganda, prejudice, and the extremes of discrimination, often targeted at cultural, ethnic and religious minorities.

Synthesis
Linking significant features of religion together in a coherent pattern – can we make sense of potential contradictions between the rights of women in secular systems like the UN and the status of women in certain religious traditions?

Application
Making the association between religions and individual, community, national and international life, identifying key religious values and their interplay with secular ones, especially in the role of NGOs.

Expression
The ability to explain the religious concepts, rituals and practices associated with women's role (or lack of role) in relation to these, and women's responses, articulating matters of deep conviction and concern through a variety of media – art, music, the novel.

Box 10.4.3

Women's rights: attitudes in religious education

Commitment
Understanding the importance of commitment to a set of values by which to live one's life.

Fairness
Considering other views carefully; a willingness to consider evidence and argument; the readiness to look beyond superficial and more deeply held prejudices against women.

Respect
Recognising in the face of prejudice and discrimination against the women, the need to respect those who have different beliefs and customs; recognising the rights of others to hold their own views, but to the extent that fundamental human rights are not abused.

Self-understanding
Developing a mature sense of self-worth and value, and developing the capacity to discern the personal relevance of religious questions to issues of gender.

continued

Enquiry
Curiosity and a desire to seek the truth; developing a personal interest in the religious and theological questions associated with gender and their ramifications in social and cultural, political and economic life.

Box 10.4.4

Women's rights: National Curriculum citizenship links

Knowledge and understanding about becoming informed citizens
1   Pupils should be taught about:
a   the legal and human rights and responsibilities underpinning society and how they relate to citizens, including the role and operation of the criminal and civil justice systems
    POSSIBLE RELIGIOUS EDUCATION LINKS: Potential conflicts between basic civil rights for women and religious traditions.
b   the origins and implications of the diverse national, regional, religious and ethnic identities in the United Kingdom and the need for mutual respect and understanding
d   the importance of playing an active part in democratic and electoral processes
e   how the economy functions, including the role of business and financial services
f   the opportunities for individuals and voluntary groups to bring about social change locally, nationally, in Europe and internationally
h   the rights and responsibilities of consumers, employers and employees
POSSIBLE RELIGIOUS EDUCATION LINKS: Attitudes of local religious communities in the United Kingdom to women's rights.

Developing skills of enquiry and communication
2   Pupils should be taught to:
a   research a topical political, spiritual, moral, social or cultural issue, problem or event by analysing information from different sources, including ICT-based sources, showing an awareness of the use and abuse of statistics
b   express, justify and defend orally and in writing a personal opinion about such issues, problems or events
c   contribute to group and exploratory class discussions, and take part in formal debates
POSSIBLE RELIGIOUS EDUCATION LINKS: See Question, discuss, research activities in Box 10.5.

Developing skills of participation and responsible action
3   Pupils should be taught to:
a   use their imagination to consider other people's experiences and be able to think about, express, explain and critically evaluate views that are not their own
b   negotiate, decide and take part responsibly in school- and community-based activities
c   reflect on the process of participating.
POSSIBLE RELIGIOUS EDUCATION LINKS: See Question, discuss, research activities in Box 10.5.

In planning for citizenship through religious education, it is crucial that neither the explicit religious education nor conscious citizenship elements of delivery are lost.

Conclusion

The notion that the rights of women – by contemporary secular standards – are not yet fully addressed within many religious traditions might yet be challenged by the traditions themselves. With Box 10.5 presenting some more focused questions, discussion points and research activities around this point, there are few debates more relevant or important to teaching citizenship through religious education.

Box 10.5

Women's rights through religious education: question, discuss, research

Question and discuss

1 Do religions oppress women?
2 Name one religious leader in the world today who is a woman. Can religious traditions truly champion women's rights if their own hierarchies are not simply unrepresentative of women (many parliaments are not) but are structurally established to prevent female participation at the highest levels?
3 How do religions justify the line of 'different but equal' to define women's roles?
4 Visit the website of the United Nations at www.un.org for the full text of the Convention on the Elimination of All Forms of Discrimination against Women, and follow links to the UN Committee on the Elimination of Discrimination against Women (CEDAW). To what extent is religion a feature of either the Convention or the Committee?
5 Women's rights have not been a major priority for religious traditions over the centuries, but then, arguably, neither have these same rights been a strong feature of any society in historical terms. (For example, women only received the vote in Switzerland in the mid-1970s.) Is it likely that religious traditions will change in relation to women's rights in the future?
6 The Church of England has permitted women priests since the early 1990s but not women bishops – what is the logic/theology here? What are the theological arguments for not allowing women a greater role in the religious hierarchy of Catholicism?
7 To what extent do male or patriarchal theologies (God defined as 'He', for example) contribute to inequitable treatment of women?

Research

8 Gender-based sexual violence has been a disturbing feature of contemporary conflict, especially in the former Yugoslavia, designed to cause maximum psychological, physical

continued

---

and emotional pain to religious minorities. Visit the international war crimes tribunal for the former Yugoslavia (www.un.org/icty).

9 Integrating gender into the agenda was an important part of the Third World Conference against Racism, Racial Discrimination, Xenophobia and Related Intolerance – www.unifem.undp.org/hr_racism. In this regard women can be doubly discriminated against – how far is religion part of the problem or part of the solution according to discussions at the conference in Johannesburg, 2002?

10 Visit the United Nations Development Fund for Women (UNIFEM) – www.unifem.undp.org. What are the particular cultural and religious issues raised by UNIFEM?

Chapter 11

The rights of indigenous peoples through religious education

Introduction

The exploitation and destruction of indigenous peoples – relatively small in number and historically powerless – have been increasingly regarded as historical marks of the arrogance of large and not exclusively western civilisations (UN 2002o, 2002p, 2002t). With a greater voice at the UN today, indigenous peoples have suffered what today we would call genocide and ethnic cleansing, as well as decimation of their languages, cultures and even habitat. Yet many such groups, including ancient tribal peoples, remain under threat today for their identity and even their very existence (Thornbury 2002). Although religious education cannot cover all traditions, and the focus on six principal religions is a matter of expediency, the rights of tribal and indigenous peoples raise important issues about the nature and extent of what it means to be a citizen in the world today.

The rights of indigenous peoples: historical-legal-political background

Indigenous, tribal or aboriginal peoples inhabit vast areas of the earth's surface, numbering according to the United Nations approximately 300 million. So-called:

> because they were living on their lands before settlers came from elsewhere; they are the descendants of those who inhabited a country or a geographical region at the time when people of different cultures or ethnic origins arrived, the new arrivals later becoming dominant through conquest, occupation, settlement or other means.

Since time immemorial, different tribal groups have competed for land and resources. Over the past five or six centuries, as Europeans began a process of colonisation, pressure on indigenous peoples intensified as never before in human history. Small but ancient groups have been historically very vulnerable in the history of colonisation. When in the mid- to late twentieth century formal colonialism began to decline, the new postcolonial States continued to exert a negative influence, almost without exception, on indigenous peoples. And today, according to the United Nations, 'Indigenous peoples belong to the poorest and most vulnerable on earth':

Although they differ among themselves in terms of economic development and the extent to which they have been able to preserve their cultural autonomy and economic independence, many indigenous societies share common characteristics. Most societies and communities have maintained their own distinct cultural traditions, and continue to speak their own languages, which are, for the most part, unwritten. As a result they have rarely completely assimilated within the national societies in which they live. Instead, they often live in subordinate positions within national societies. They generally inhabit marginal and inhospitable territories. Many of them survive through hunting and gathering and/or practising pastoralism or subsistence farming.

Despite these common characteristics, there does not exist any single accepted definition of indigenous peoples that captures their diversity. Therefore, self-identification as indigenous or tribal group is a fundamental criterion for determining whether groups are indigenous or tribal, sometimes in combination with other variables such as 'language spoken' and 'geographic location or concentration'.

(UN 2002p)

Indigenous peoples are represented on most of the planet's continents, and many risk disappearance. Box 11.1 provides an indication of some of the international standards put in place to protect such peoples (see also Meijknecht 2001).

Box 11.1

International legal standards: defending the rights of indigenous peoples

Right of self-determination
Declaration on the Granting of Independence to Colonial Countries and Peoples (14 December 1960)
General Assembly resolution 1803 (XVII) of 14 December 1962, 'Permanent sovereignty over natural resources' (14 December 1962)

Prevention of discrimination
Equal Remuneration Convention (29 June 1951, into effect 23 May 1953)
Discrimination (Employment and Occupation) Convention (15 June 1960)
Convention against Discrimination in Education (14 December 1960)
Protocol Instituting a Conciliation and Good Offices Commission to be responsible for seeking a settlement of any disputes which may arise between States Parties to the Convention against Discrimination in Education (10 June 1962, into effect 24 October 1968)
United Nations Declaration on the Elimination of All Forms of Racial Discrimination (20 December 1962)
International Convention on the Elimination of All Forms of Racial Discrimination (21 December 1965)

continued

International Convention on the Suppression and Punishment of the Crime of *Apartheid* (30 November 1973)
Declaration on Race and Racial Prejudice (27 November 1978)
Declaration on the Elimination of All Forms of Intolerance and of Discrimination based on Religion or Belief (25 November 1981)
Declaration on the Rights of Persons Belonging to National or Ethnic, Religious and Linguistic Minorities (18 December 1992)

Employment
ILO Convention (No. 169) concerning Indigenous and Tribal Peoples in Independent Countries (21 June 1989, into effect 5 September 1991)

For full texts of these documents, follow links at www.un.unhchr.org

---

The most significant piece of, as yet draft, legislation is the UN Draft Declaration on Indigenous and Tribal Rights (1994) (see Gayim 1994), critical sections of which are summarised in Box 11.2.

Box 11.2

UN Draft Declaration on Indigenous and Tribal Rights (1994)

PART I
Article 1 states that 'Indigenous peoples have the right to the full and effective enjoyment of all human rights and fundamental freedoms recognized in the Charter of the United Nations, the Universal Declaration of Human Rights and international human rights law.'
Article 2 states that 'Indigenous individuals and peoples are free and equal to all other individuals and peoples in dignity and rights, and have the right to be free from any kind of adverse discrimination, in particular that based on their indigenous origin or identity.'
Article 3 states that 'Indigenous peoples have the right of self-determination. By virtue of that right they freely determine their political status and freely pursue their economic, social and cultural development.'
Article 4 states that 'Indigenous peoples have the right to maintain and strengthen their distinct political, economic, social and cultural characteristics, as well as their legal systems, while retaining their rights to participate fully, if they so choose, in the political, economic, social and cultural life of the State.'
Article 5 states that 'Every indigenous individual has the right to a nationality.'

continued

PART II
Article 6 states that 'Indigenous peoples have the collective right to live in freedom, peace and security as distinct peoples and to full guarantees against genocide or any other act of violence, including the removal of indigenous children from their families and communities under any pretext.'
Article 7 states that 'Indigenous peoples have the collective and individual right not to be subjected to ethnocide and cultural genocide', this to include redress for such action directed against them.
Article 8 states that 'Indigenous peoples have the collective and individual right to maintain and develop their distinct identities and characteristics, including the right to identify themselves as indigenous and to be recognized as such.'
Article 9 states that 'Indigenous peoples and individuals have the right to belong to an indigenous community or nation, in accordance with the traditions and customs of the community or nation concerned. No disadvantage of any kind may arise from the exercise of such a right.'
Article 10 states that 'Indigenous peoples shall not be forcibly removed from their lands or territories. No relocation shall take place without the free and informed consent of the indigenous peoples concerned and after agreement on just and fair compensation and, where possible, with the option of return.'
Article 11 states that 'Indigenous peoples have the right to special protection and security in periods of armed conflict.'

PART III
Article 12 states that 'Indigenous peoples have the right to practise and revitalize their cultural traditions and customs.' This includes 'the right to maintain, protect and develop the past, present and future manifestations of their cultures, such as archaeological and historical sites, artefacts, designs, ceremonies, technologies and visual and performing arts and literature'. It also includes 'the right to the restitution of cultural, intellectual, religious and spiritual property taken without their free and informed consent or in violation of their laws, traditions and customs'.
Article 13 states that 'Indigenous peoples have the right to manifest, practise, develop and teach their spiritual and religious traditions, customs and ceremonies; the right to maintain, protect, and have access in privacy to their religious and cultural sites; the right to the use and control of ceremonial objects; and the right to the repatriation of human remains.' This article also recognises States' responsibilities to preserve, respect and protect sacred indigenous sites.
Article 14 states that 'Indigenous peoples have the right to revitalize, use, develop and transmit to future generations their histories, languages, oral traditions, philosophies, writing systems and literatures, and to designate and retain their own names for communities, places and persons.'

For the full text, follow links at www.unhchr.org

The United Nations Declaration on the Rights of Indigenous Peoples represents one of the most important developments in the promotion and protection of their basic rights and fundamental freedoms. The Declaration also foresees mutually acceptable and fair procedures for resolving conflicts between indigenous peoples and powerful nation-states. It constitutes the minimum standards for the survival and well-being of the world's indigenous peoples.

Box 11.3 provides some key links to the UN and indigenous and tribal peoples.

Box 11.3

The rights of indigenous peoples: UN links

Office of the High Commissioner for Human Rights
www.unhchr.ch

Indigenous Populations and/or Minorities
www.ifad.org/evaluation/public_html/eksyst/doc/lle/themes/ipm

International Labour Organization (ILO) – Geneva, Switzerland
www.ilo.org

International Labour Standards and Human Rights
www.ilo.org/public/english/standards/norm/index

ILOLEX database
ilolex.ilo.ch:1567/public/english/50normes/infleg/iloeng/index

Research documents
The Search For Identity Ethnicity Religion and Political Violence
www.unrisd.org/engindex/publ/list/op/op6/op06–03

Ethnic Violence Conflict Resolution and Cultural Pluralism
www.unrisd.org/engindex/publ/list/conf/eth1/eth1–04

Ethnic Diversity and Public Policy: An Overview
www.unrisd.org/engindex/publ/list/op/op8/op08–05

United Nations Educational, Scientific and Cultural Organization (UNESCO) – Paris, France
www.unesco.org

Multiculturalism
www.unesco.org/most/most1

continued

Linguistic rights
www.unesco.org/most/ln1

Religious rights
www.unesco.org/most/rr1

Cultural heritage
www.unesco.org/culture/heritage

Intercultural dialogue and pluralism
www.unesco.org/culture/dial_eng

United Nations documents and studies on indigenous issues
www.unhchr.ch.huridocda/huridoca.nsf

However, the protection of the rights of indigenous peoples presents particular problems. There is often a conflict between the economic needs of growing populations in the 'mainstream' of nation-states, especially the need for basic development, and protection of the environment of tribal peoples. In the developed world, there is great pressure to protect the remaining wilderness of the world. Indigenous peoples do not always see the issue of land use and environmental conservation in the same way (Wade 2001; Grim 2001).

In 1992, the United Nations endorsed a study on measures that should be taken by the international community to strengthen respect for the cultural and intellectual property of indigenous peoples. The study completed by the Economic and Social Council was submitted to the Sub-Commission on Human Rights in August 1993. It is regarded as the 'first formal step in responding to the concerns expressed by indigenous peoples and as a basis for appropriate standard-setting to provide them with some immediate relief from the widespread and growing threats to the integrity of their cultural, spiritual, artistic, religious and scientific traditions'.

The rights of indigenous peoples through religious education: planning notes

Given the foregoing historical-legal-political background, what we need to do as religious educators is integrate the key aspects of the rights of indigenous peoples appropriate to a religious education context. This means identifying the explicit religious context and planning for explicitly religious education learning outcomes. While presenting particular lesson plans might be prescriptive, what is offered here – adapting the structure of the QCA *Model Syllabuses for Religious Education* – is a suggested typology (Boxes 11.4.1 to 11.4.3), identifying:

- Attainment targets in religious education
- Skills and processes in religious education
- Attitudes in religious education

What follows (Box 11.4.4) is a series of suggested links for this theme to National Curriculum citizenship.

Box 11.4.1

Indigenous rights: attainment targets in religious education

Attainment target 1: Learning about religions

Identify a critical period in the history of genocide and give an account of the cultural, ethnic and/or religious involvement and/or response to events – the Holocaust, Rwanda, the former Yugoslavia.

Explore religious language, stories and symbolism that enable an individual or a people to come to terms with genocide.

Attainment target 2: Learning from religions

Give an informed and considered response to the religious and moral issues surrounding the individual and collective human suffering behind the statistical horrors of genocide.

Reflect on what might be learned – if anything can be learned – from genocide in the light of one's own beliefs and experience.

Identify and respond to questions of meaning with which genocide confronts humanity.

Box 11.4.2

Indigenous rights: skills and processes in religious education

Investigation

Knowing how to use different types of sources as a way of gathering information about tribal and indigenous peoples.

Knowing what may constitute evidence for understanding the decimation suffered by indigenous peoples often at the hands of global religions associated with great economic and military powers, historically and today.

continued

Interpretation
The ability to draw from artefacts, works of art, poetry and symbolism of indigenous peoples.

Reflection
The ability to reflect on the feelings, relationships, experience, ultimate questions, beliefs and practices of indigenous peoples.

Empathy
The ability to consider the thoughts, feelings, experiences, attitudes, beliefs and values of indigenous peoples.

Evaluation
The ability to debate issues of religious significance with reference to evidence from ethnographic and other sources.

Analysis
Distinguishing between opinion, belief and fact, especially in assessments of propaganda, prejudice, and the extremes of discrimination, often targeted at cultural, ethnic and religious minorities such as tribal and indigenous peoples.

Synthesis
Linking significant features of religion together in a coherent pattern – celebrating diversity in tribal and indigenous identity.

Application
Making the association between religions and individual, community, national and international life, identifying key religious values and their interplay with secular ones, especially in the role of NGOs and indigenous peoples.

Expression
The ability to explain the persistence of concepts, rituals and practices associated with indigenous religions, and their particular cultural articulation of matters of deep conviction and ancient historical concerns through a variety of media – art, music, the novel.

Box 11.4.3

Indigenous rights: attitudes in religious education

Commitment
Understanding the importance of commitment to a set of values by which to live one's life, and the pressure that minority, tribal and indigenous traditions experience from the forces of global change, pressures that threaten their very survival.

Fairness
Considering other views carefully; a willingness to consider evidence and argument; the readiness to look beyond surface impressions to signs of hope, truth, remembrance and eventual reconciliation.

Respect
Recognising in the face of genocide the need to respect those who have different beliefs and customs; recognising the rights of others to hold their own views; the avoidance of ridicule; and the discernment of what is worthy of respect and what is not.

Self-understanding
Developing a mature sense of self-worth and value; developing the capacity to discern the personal relevance of religious questions, and relative good fortune.

Enquiry
A desire to seek the truth in the history of colonial and postcolonial relations of powerful States and global religions with indigenous peoples.

Box 11.4.4

The rights of indigenous peoples through religious education: National Curriculum citizenship links

Knowledge and understanding about becoming informed citizens
1 Pupils should be taught about:
i   the United Kingdom's relations in Europe, including the European Union, and relations with the Commonwealth and the United Nations
j   the wider issues and challenges of global interdependence and responsibility, including sustainable development and Local Agenda 21
POSSIBLE RELIGIOUS EDUCATION LINKS: Colonial and Commonwealth relations; the marginalisation of minority traditions within religious education.

continued

Developing skills of enquiry and communication

2   Pupils should be taught to:

a   research a topical political, spiritual, moral, social or cultural issue, problem or event by analysing information from different sources, including ICT-based sources, showing an awareness of the use and abuse of statistics

b   express, justify and defend orally and in writing a personal opinion about such issues, problems or events

c   contribute to group and exploratory class discussions, and take part in formal debates

POSSIBLE RELIGIOUS EDUCATION LINKS: See Question, discuss, research activities in Box 11.5.

Developing skills of participation and responsible action

3   Pupils should be taught to:

a   use their imagination to consider other people's experiences and be able to think about, express, explain and critically evaluate views that are not their own

b   negotiate, decide and take part responsibly in school- and community-based activities

c   reflect on the process of participating

POSSIBLE RELIGIOUS EDUCATION LINKS: See Question, discuss, research activities in Box 11.5.

Conclusion

Although teaching about and learning from the precarious nature of global citizenship shared by indigenous peoples is never likely to be a major part of the religious education curriculum, it has the potential to extend the subject's range beyond the major six traditions. With Box 11.5 raising related questions, for the religious educator teaching citizenship it will also mean the re-examination of those histories of evangelisation that took well-intentioned missionaries to places distant from Europe to convert and to save.

Box 11.5

The rights of indigenous peoples through religious education: question, discuss, research

Question and discuss

1   Some traditions, notably Christianity, in the history of western imperial expansion have been complicit in processes of colonialism. Is this something that should concern Christians today? Should such histories have a more prominent part in religious education?

continued

2 In terms of sheer brutality, indigenous peoples have suffered immense decimation even to the point of genocide. In this context can missionary activity to tribal peoples still be justified?

3 The QCA model syllabuses, following the 1988 Education Reform Act, outline the teaching of Christianity and 'the other principal religions represented in Great Britain'. With contemporary models of citizenship emphasising equal rights for all, is this notion of otherness appropriate?

4 Is the study of the six major world religions (and six only) a form of religious imperialism?

5 Does the study of indigenous and tribal peoples have any role in Britain, Europe or any developed nation?

Research

6 Visit www.survival-international.org What are the governing principles of the organisation? What educational resources are available there that might be applied to religious education?

References

Addo, Michael K. (ed.) (1999) *Human Rights Standards and the Responsibilities of Transnational Corporations* (London: Kluwer).

Agosin, Marjorie (ed.) (2001) *Women, Gender and Human Rights: A Global Perspective* (New Brunswick: NJ: Rutgers University Press).

Ahier, J., J. Beck and R. Moore (2002) *Graduate Citizens: Issues of Citizenship and Higher Education* (London: Routledge).

Allen, Michael Thad (2002) *The Business of Genocide: The SS, Slave Labour and the Concentration Camps* (Chapel Hill, NC: University of North Carolina Press).

American Library Association (2002) *Intellectual Freedom Manual* (Washington: Office for Intellectual Freedom of the American Library Association).

Askin, Kelly D. and Dorean M. Koenig (eds) (2000) *Women and International Human Rights Law* (Ardsley, NY: Transnational).

Atkin, Bill and Katrina Evans (eds) (2000) *Human Rights and the Common Good: Christian Perspectives* (Wellington, NZ: Victoria University Press).

Audit Commission (2000) *Another Country: Implementing Dispersal under the Immigration and Asylum Act 1999* (London: Audit Commission).

Ayton-Shenker, Diana (1995) *The Challenge of Human Rights and Cultural Diversity* (Geneva: UN Department of Public Information).

Bales, Kevin (2000) *Disposable People* (Berkeley: University of California Press).

Ball, Howard (1999) *Prosecuting War Crimes and Genocide: The Twentieth-Century Experience* (Lawrence: University Press of Kansas).

Bartov, Omer and Phyllis Mack (eds) (2001) *In God's Name: Genocide and Religion in the Twentieth Century* (Oxford: Berghahn).

Beigbeder, Yves (2001) *New Challenges for UNICEF: Children, Women and Human Rights* (Basingstoke: Palgrave).

Bendell, Jem (ed.) (2000) *Terms for Endearment: Business, NGOs and Sustainable Development* (Sheffield: Greenleaf).

Best, R. (1999) 'The Impact of a Decade of Educational Change on Pastoral Care and PSE: A Survey of Teachers' Perceptions', *Pastoral Care in Education* 17(2): 3–13.

Best, R. (2002) *Pastoral Care and Personal-Social Education: A Review of UK Research Undertaken for the British Educational Research Association* (Southwell, Notts: BERA).

Best, R., P. Lang, C. Lodge and C. Watkins (eds) (1995) *Pastoral Care and Personal-Social Education* (London: Cassell).

Bloom, Irene, J. Paul Martin and Wayne L. Proudfoot (eds) (2000) *Religious Diversity and Human Rights* (New York: Columbia University Press).

Brown, Alan (2000) 'The Chichester Project: Teaching Christianity: A World Religions Approach', in Michael Grimmitt (ed.) *Pedagogies of Religious Education: Case Studies in the Research and Development of Good Pedagogic Practice* (Great Wakering: McCrimmons), 53–69.

Brown, Lester R. (2001) *State of the World 2001: Progress Towards a Sustainable Society* (London: Earthscan).

Brown, Michael E. (ed.) (2001) *Nationalism and Ethnic Conflict* (Cambridge, MA: MIT Press).

Cahil, Kevin M. (1999) *A Framework for Survival: Health, Human Rights and Humanitarian Assistance in Conflicts and Disasters* (London: Routledge).

Carisnaes, Walter, Thomas Risse and Beth A. Simmons (eds) (2002) *Handbook of International Relations* (London: Sage).

Casanova, J. (1994) *Public Religions in the Modern World* (Chicago: Chicago University Press).

CEM (2000) *What the Churches Say on Moral and Social Issues* (Derby: Christian Education Movement).

Chandler, David P. (2001) *Voices from S-21: Terror and History in Pol Pot's Secret Prison* (Berkeley: University of California Press).

Charny, Israel W. (ed.) (1999) *Encyclopedia of Genocide*, forewords by Desmond M. Tutu and Simon Weisenthal (Santa Barbara, CA: ABC-CLIO).

Chorbajian, Levon and George Shirnian (eds) (1999) *Studies in Comparative Genocide* (Basingstoke: Macmillan).

Clement, John (ed.) (1998) *Human Rights and the Churches* (Geneva: World Council of Churches).

Conway, Martin and Jose Gotovitch (eds) (2002) *Europe in Exile: European Exile Communities in Britain 1940–1945* (Oxford: Berghahn).

Cooling, Trevor (2000) 'The Stapleford Project: Theology as the Basis for Religious Education', in Michael Grimmitt (ed.) *Pedagogies of Religious Education: Case Studies in the Research and Development of Good Pedagogic Practice* (Great Wakering: McCrimmons), 153–69.

Copley, Terence (1997) *Teaching Religion: Fifty Years of Religious Education in England and Wales* (Exeter: Exeter University Press).

Copley, Terence (2000) *Spiritual Development in the State School* (Exeter: Exeter University Press).

Crick, B. (1998) *Education for Citizenship and the Teaching of Democracy in Schools: Final Report of the Advisory Group on Citizenship* (London: QCA).

Crick, B. (2000) *Essays on Citizenship* (London: Continuum).

Dadrian, Vahakn N. (1999) *Warrant for Genocide: Key Elements of Turko-Armenian Conflict* (New Brunswick, NJ: Transaction Publishers).

Davies, L. (1999) 'Comparing Definitions of Democracy in Education', *Compare* 29(2): 127–40.

Davies, L. (2000) *Citizenship Education and Human Rights Education: Key Concepts and Debates* (London: British Council).

Davis, David Brion (2001) *In the Image of God: Religion, Moral Values and Our Heritage of Slavery* (New Haven: Yale University Press).

de Baets, Antoon (2002) *Censorship of Historical Thought: A World Guide, 1945–2000* (Westport and London: Greenwood Press).

DfEE (1999) *The National Curriculum for England: Citizenship* (London: Department for Education and Employment and the Qualifications and Curriculum Authority).

DfID (2000) *Halving World Poverty by 2015* (London: Department for International Development).

DfEE (2000) *Holocaust Memorial Day: Remembering Genocides, Lessons for the Future Education Pack* (London: Department for Education and Employment).

Edmonds, D. and J. Eidinow (2001) *Wittgenstein's Poker: The Story of a Ten Minute Argument Between Two Great Philosophers* (London: Faber and Faber).

Engerman, Stanley, Seymour Drescher and Robert Paquette (eds) (2000) *Slavery*, Oxford Readers Series (Oxford: Oxford University Press).

Fish, Stanley (1999) *The Trouble with Principle* (Cambridge, MA: Harvard University Press).

Flew, A. (2000) *Education for Citizenship*

Forsythe, David P. (2000) *Human Rights in International Relations*, 3rd edn (Cambridge: Cambridge University Press).

Fukuyama, Francis (1992) *The End of History and the Last Man* (Harmondsworth: Penguin).

Gayim, Eyassu (1994) *The UN Draft Declaration on Indigenous Peoples: Assessment of the Draft Prepared by the Working Group on Indigenous Populations* (Rovaniemi: University of Lapland).

Gearon, L. (2000) 'The Imagined Other: Postcolonial Theory and Religious Education', *British Journal of Religious Education* 23(2): 98–106.

Gearon, L. (2001) 'Some Postcolonial Perspectives on Children's Spirituality in a World of Violence', in J. Erricker, C. Ota and C. Erricker (eds) *Spiritual Education: Cultural, Religious and Social Differences* (Brighton: Sussex Academic Press), 219–32.

Gearon, L. (ed.) (2002) *Human Rights and Religion: A Reader* (Brighton and Portland: Sussex Academic Press).

Gearon, L. (2003a) *How Do We Learn to Become Good Citizens? A Professional User Review of UK Research* (London: British Educational Research Association).

Gearon, L. (ed.) (2003b) *Learning to Teach Citizenship in the Secondary School* (London: RoutledgeFalmer).

Giddens, A. (1998) *The Third Way: The Renewal of Social Democracy* (London: Polity Press).

Glancy, Jennifer A. (2001) *Slavery in Early Christianity* (Oxford: Oxford University Press).

Gourevitch, Philip (1999) *We Wish to Inform You That Tomorrow We Will Be Killed With Our Families: Stories from Rwanda* (London: Picador).

Grim, John A. (ed.) (2001) *Indigenous Traditions and Ecology: The Interbeing of Cosmology and Community* (Cambridge, MA: Harvard University Press).

Grimmitt, Michael (ed.) (2000) *Pedagogies of Religious Education: Case Studies in the Research and Development of Good Pedagogic Practice in RE* (Great Wakering: McCrimmons).

Gustafson, Carrie and Peter Juviler (eds) (1999) *Religion and Human Rights: Competing Claims* (London: M. E. Sharpe).

Halstead, M. and M. Taylor (2000) 'Learning and Teaching about Values: A Review of Recent Literature', *Cambridge Journal of Education* 10(2): 169–202.

Halstead, M. and M. Taylor (2001) *A Review of Values Education* (Slough: NFER).

Hamel, Pierre (ed.) (2001) *Globalization and Social Movements* (Basingstoke: Palgrave).

Harlow, B. and M. Carter (eds) (1999) *Imperialism and Orientalism: A Documentary Sourcebook* (Oxford: Blackwell).

Harmer, H.J.P. (ed.) (2001) *The Longman Companion to Slavery, Emancipation and Civil Rights* (Harlow: Longman).

Hart, R. (1997) *Children's Participation: The Theory and Practice of Involving Young Citizens in Community Development and Environmental Care* (London: Earthscan Publications).

Hastings, Adrian (1999) *A World History of Christianity* (London: Cassell).

Haydon, Graham (1999) 'Violence and the Demand for Moral Education', *Journal of Philosophy of Education* 33: 1–156.

Hayfield, Celia (2001) *Signposts: Information for Asylum Seekers and Refugees* (London: National Information Forum).

Haynes, J. (1998) *Religion in Global Politics* (London: Longman).

Haynes, J. (2000) 'Religion', in Brian White, Richard Little and Michael Smith (eds) *Issues in Global Politics*, 2nd edn (Basingstoke: Palgrave).

Haynes, Stephen R. (2002) *Noah's Curse: The Biblical Justification of American Slavery* (Oxford: Oxford University Press).

Heater, D. (1999). *What is Citizenship?* (Cambridge: Polity Press).

Helton, Arthur C. (2002) *The Price of Indifference: Refugees and Humanitarian Action in the New Century* (Oxford: Oxford University Press).

Hinton, Alexander Laban (ed.) (2002) *Genocide: An Anthropological Reader* (Malden, MA: Blackwell Publishers).

Hogan, Linda (1998) *Christian Perspectives on Development Issues* (London: Cafod).

Home Office (2000) *The Human Rights Act. Guidance for Public Authorities* (London: Human Rights Unit).

Horowitz, David (2002) *Uncivil War: The Controversy over Reparations for Slavery* (San Francisco, CA: Encounter Books).

Howland, Courtney (1999) *Religious Fundamentalisms and the Human Rights of Women* (Basingstoke: Macmillan).

HRW (2001a) 'No Safe Refuge: The Impact of the September 11 Attacks on Refugees, Asylum Seekers and Migrants in the Afghanistan Region and Worldwide' (New York: HRW).

HRW (2001b) 'Anti-Racism Summit Ends on Hopeful Note' (New York: Human Rights Watch).

HRW (2002) *International Trafficking of Women and Children* (New York: Human Rights Watch).

Human Rights Centre (2000) *Key Points on Women's Human Rights: An Initiative of the Study Group on Women's Human Rights* (Colchester: Human Rights Centre, University of Essex).

Huntington, S. (1993) *The Clash of Civilizations* (Washington, DC: American Enterprise Institute).

International Association for Religious Freedom (2001) *Centennial Reflections International Association for Religious Freedom, 1900–2000* (Assen, the Netherlands: Van Gorcum).

Jackson, R. (1997) *Religious Education: An Interpretive Approach* (London: Hodder and Stoughton).

Jackson, Robert (2000) 'The Warwick Religious Education Project: The Interpretive Approach to Religious Education', in Michael Grimmitt (ed.) *Pedagogies of Religious Education: Case Studies in the Research and Development of Good Pedagogic Practice* (Great Wakering: McCrimmons), 130–52.

Jackson, R. (2002) *International Perspectives on Citizenship, Education and Religious Diversity* (London: RoutledgeFalmer).

Jeffries, Alison (ed.) (1999) *Women's Voices, Women's Rights*, Oxford Amnesty Lectures (Oxford: Westview).

Johnson, M. Glen and Janusz Symonides (eds) (1999) *The Universal Declaration of Human Rights: A History of Its Creation and Implementation 1948–1998* (Paris: UNESCO).

Jones, Derek (2001) *Censorship: A World Encyclopedia* (London: Fitzroy Dearborn).

Karolides, Nicholas J., Margaret Bald and Dawn B. Sova (eds) (1999) *100 Banned Books: Censorship Histories of World Literature* (New York: Checkmark Books).

Keast, J. (2000) 'Citizenship and RE', *RE Today* (Derby: CEM).

Keekok, Lee, Alan Holland and Desmond McNeill (eds) (2000) *Global Sustainable Development in the Twenty-First Century* (Edinburgh: Edinburgh University Press).

Kerr, D. (2003) 'Citizenship: Local, National, International', in L. Gearon (ed.) *Learning to Teach Citizenship in the Secondary School* (London: RoutledgeFalmer).

Kliot, Nurit and David Newman (eds) *Geopolitics at the End of the Twentieth Century* (London: F. Cass).

Kressel, Neil J. (2001) *Mass Hate: The Global Rise of Genocide and Terror* (Cambridge, MA: Westview).

Kumar, Krishna (ed.) (2001) *Women and Civil War: Impact, Organizations and Action* (Boulder and London: Lynne Rienner Publishers).

Kung, Hans (1995) 'A Global Ethic and Education', *British Journal of Religious Education* 18(1): 6–21.

Kung, Hans and H. Schmidt (eds) (1998) *The Declaration of the Parliament of the World's Religions*, in *A Global Ethic and Global Responsibilities: Two Declarations* (London: SCM).

Langley, Winston (ed.) (1999) *Encyclopedia of Human Rights Issues Since 1945* (London: Fitzroy Dearborn).

Laqueur, Walter (2001) *Generation Exodus: The Fate of Young Jewish Refugees from Nazi Germany* (Hanover, NH: Brandeis University Press).

Lawton, D., J. Cairns and R. Gardner (2000) *Education for Citizenship*

Leckie, David and Pickersgill, David (1999) *The 1998 Human Rights Act Explained* (London: Stationery Office).

Lerner, Nathan (2000) *Religion, Beliefs, and Human Rights* (Maryknoll, NY: Orbis).

Lorey, David E. and William H. Beezley (eds) (2002) *Genocide, Collective Violence and Popular Memory: The Politics of Remembrance in the Twentieth Century* (Wilmington, DE: SR Books).

Lyotard, J.-F. (1984) *The Postmodern Condition* (Manchester: Manchester University Press).

McColgan, Aileen (2000) *Women under the Law: The False Promise of Human Rights* (Harlow: Longman).

MacIntyre, Alastair (1985) *After Virtue*, 2nd edn (London: Duckworth).

MacIntyre, Alastair (1988) *Whose Justice? Which Rationality?* (London: Duckworth).

McLaughlin, T.H. (1992) 'Citizenship, Diversity and Education: A Philosophical Perspective', *Journal of Moral Education* 21(3): 235–50.

McLaughlin, T.H. (2000) 'Citizenship Education in England: The Crick Report and Beyond', *Journal of Philosophy of Education* 34(4): 541–70.

Magee, B. (1985) *Popper*, 3rd edn (London: Fontana).

Mansell, Wade (1999) in D. Bell (ed.) *Teaching Human Rights* (Warwick: Warwick Legal Centre).

Marshall, Paul (ed.) (2000) *Religious Freedom in the World* (Nashville: Broadman and Holman).

Mawson, Andrew, Rebecca Dodd and John Hilary (2000) *War Brought Us Here: Protecting Children Displaced within Their Own Countries by Conflict* (London: Save the Children).

Medawar, J.S. (2000) *Hitler's Gift: Scientists Who Fled Nazi Germany* (London: Piatkus).

Meijknecht, Anna (2001) *Towards International Personality: The Position of Minorities and Indigenous Peoples in International Law* (Antwerpen: Intersentia-Hart).

Mills, Kurt (1998) *Human Rights in the Emerging Global Order: A New Sovereignty?* (Basingstoke: Macmillan).

Morsinky, Johannes (1999) *The Universal Declaration of Human Rights: Origins and Intent* (Philadelphia: University of Pennsylvania Press).

Mostyn, Trevor (2002) *Censorship in Islamic Societies* (London: Saqi).

Nitze, Paul (ed.) (2002) *Human Rights Report on Trafficking in Persons, Especially Women and Children: A Country-by-Country Report On a Contemporary Form of Slavery / The Protection Project* (Washington, DC: Johns Hopkins University Press).

Organisation for Economic Co-operation and Development (2000) *The Creative Society of the 21st Century* (Paris: OECD).

Osler, Audrey (2001) *Citizenship Education: The Global Dimension* (London: Development Education Association).

Popper, K. (1945) *The Open Society and Its Enemies*, 2 vols (London: Routledge & Kegan Paul).

Popper, K. (1986) *Unended Quest: An Intellectual Biography* (London: Flamingo).

Prince, Baden, Jill Rutter and Marie Kerrigan (2002) *Handbook of Education for Refugees* (Stoke-on-Trent: Trentham).

QCA (1998a) *Model Syllabus for Religious Education 1* (London: Qualifications and Curriculum Authority).

QCA (1998b) *Model Syllabus for Religious Education 2* (London: Qualifications and Curriculum Authority).

QCA (1998c) *Final Report of the Advisory Group on Citizenship* (London: Qualifications and Curriculum Authority).

QCA (2000a) *Religious Education: A Scheme of Work for Key Stages 1 and 2* (London: Qualifications and Curriculum Authority).

QCA (2000b) *Initial Guidance on Citizenship* (London: Qualifications and Curriculum Authority).

QCA (2001a) *Religious Education: A Scheme of Work for Key Stage 3* (London: QCA).

QCA (2001b) *Citizenship: Key Stages 3–4* (London: Qualifications and Curriculum Authority).

QCA (2001c) *Citizenship: A Scheme of Work for Key Stage 3: Teachers Guide* (London: Qualifications and Curriculum Authority).

QCA (2001d) *Citizenship: A Scheme of Work for Key Stage 4: Teachers Guide* (London: Qualifications and Curriculum Authority).

QCA (2001e) *Citizenship: A Scheme of Work for Key Stage 3* (London: Qualifications and Curriculum Authority).

QCA (2001f) *Citizenship: A Scheme of Work for Key Stage 4* (London: Qualifications and Curriculum Authority).

QCA (2001g) *Getting Involved: Extending Opportunities for Pupil Participation (KS3)* (London: Qualifications and Curriculum Authority).

QCA (2001h) *Staying Involved: Extending Opportunities for Pupil Participation (KS4)* (London: Qualifications and Curriculum Authority).

Reed, Charles (ed.) (2001) *Development Matters: Christian Perspectives on Globalization* (London: Church House Publishing).

Refugee Council (1996) *Killing Me Slowly: Refugees and Torture* (London: Refugee Council).

Refugee Council (1997) *Changing Lives: Stories of Exile* ((London: Refugee Council).

Refugee Council (1998) *Cost of Survival: Trafficking of Refugees in the UK* (London: Refugee Council).

Refugee Council (2001) *Sri Lanka: Human Rights and Refugee Returns* (London: Refugee Council).

Refugee Council (2002a) *Refugees and Progression Routes to Employment* (London: Refugee Council).

Refugee Council (2002b) *Where are the Children?* (London: Refugee Council).

Refugee Council (2002c) *Credit to the Nation* (London: Refugee Council).

Refugee Council/Oxfam (2002) *Poverty and Asylum in the UK* (London: Refugee Council).

Rendel, Margherita (1997) *Whose Human Rights?* (London: Trentham).

Robertson, David (1997) *A Dictionary of Human Rights* (London: Europa Publications).

Robinson, Jenny (ed.) (2001) *Development and Displacement* (Oxford: Open University and Oxford University Press).

Roddick, Anita (2001) *Take It Personally: How Globalisation Affects You and How to Fight Back* (London: Thorsons).

Rohrbach, Augusta (2002) *Truth Stranger than Fiction: Race, Realism and the US Literary Marketplace* (Basingstoke: Palgrave).

Rorty, Richard (1989) *Contingency, Irony and Solidarity* (Cambridge: Cambridge University Press).

Rosenbaum, Alan S. (ed.) (2001) *Is the Holocaust Unique? Perspectives on Comparative Genocide* (Oxford: Westview).

Rudge, John (2000) 'The Westhill Project: Religious Education as Maturing Pupils: Patterns of Belief and Behaviour', in Michael Grimmitt (ed.) *Pedagogies of Religious Education: Case Studies in the Research and Development of Good Pedagogic Practice* (Great Wakering: McCrimmons), 88–111.

Ryan, Stephen (2000) *The United Nations and International Politics* (London: Macmillan).

Ryan, Stephen (2002) 'The United Nations', in L. Gearon (ed.) *Human Rights and Religion: A Reader* (Brighton and Portland: Sussex Academic Press).

Schabas, William (2000) *Genocide in International Law: The Crime of Crimes* (Cambridge: Cambridge University Press).

Schechter, Michael G. (ed.) (2001) *United Nations-Sponsored World Conferences: Focus on Impact and Follow-Up* (Tokyo: United Nations University Press).

Sellar, Kirsten (2002) *The Rise and Rise of Human Rights* (London: Sutton).

Shaw, Brent (ed.) (2001) *Spartacus and the Slave Wars: A Brief History with Documents* (Boston, MA: Bedford).

Shepherd, Verene A. (2002) *Working Slavery, Pricing Freedom: Perspectives from the Caribbean, Africa and the African Diaspora* (Oxford: James Currey).

Smart, Ninian (1989) *The World's Religions* (Cambridge: Cambridge University Press).

Smith, Helmut Walser (ed.) (2002) *The Holocaust and Other Genocides: History, Representation, Ethics* (Nashville: Vanderbilt University Press).

Stahnke, Tad and J. Paul Martin (eds) (1998) *Religion and Human Rights: Basic Documents* (New York: Columbia University Press/Center for the Study of Human Rights).

Steele, Philip (2000) *Freedom of Speech* (London: Watts).

Steiner, Niklaus (2000) *Arguing About Asylum: The Complexity of Refugee Debates in Europe* (New York and London: St Martin's Press).

Tackach, James (ed.) (2001) *Slave Narratives* (San Diego, CA: Greenhaven).

Tanaka, Toshiuki (2001) *Japan's Comfort Women: Sexual Slavery and Prostitution during World War II and the US Occupation* (New York: Routledge).

Taylor, Monica J. (1999) *Citizenship Education in the UK: An Overview* (Slough: NFER).

Thornbury, Patrick (2002) *Indigenous Peoples and Human Rights* (Manchester: Manchester University Press).

UN (1993) *World Conference on Human Rights: The Vienna Declaration and Programme of Action* (New York: United Nations).

UN (1998) *Review of Vienna Statement by the United Nations High Commissioner for Human Rights* (New York: United Nations).

UN (2000) *The World's Women, 2000: Trends and Statistics* (New York: United Nations).

UN (2002a) *Civil and Political Rights*, Fact Sheet 15 (New York: United Nations).

UN (2002b) *The Committee on Economic, Social and Cultural Rights* (New York: United Nations).

UN (2002c) *Discrimination against Women: The Convention and the Committee* (New York: United Nations).

UN (2002d) *Elimination of All Forms of Intolerance and Discrimination Based on Religion or Belief*, Human Rights Study Series, No. 2 (New York: United Nations).

UN (2002e) *Extrajudicial, Summary or Arbitrary Executions*, Fact Sheet 11 (New York: United Nations).

UN (2002f) *Fact Sheet on Modern Slavery* (New York: United Nations).

UN (2002g) *Harmful Traditional Practices Affecting the Health of Women and Children*, Fact Sheet 23 (New York: United Nations).

UN (2002h) *Human Rights: A Compilation of International Instruments*, vol. I, parts I and II (New York: United Nations).

UN (2002i) *Human Rights: A Compilation of International Instruments – Regional Instruments*, Vol. II (New York: United Nations).

UN (2002j) *Human Rights and Refugees*, Fact Sheet 20 (New York: United Nations).

UN (2002k) *The Impact of Mercenary Activities on the Right of Peoples to Self-Determination*, Fact Sheet 28 (New York: United Nations).

UN (2002l) *Internally Displaced Persons: Compilation and Analysis of Legal Norms*, Human Rights Study Series, No. 9 (New York: United Nations).

UN (2002m) *International Bill of Human Rights*, Fact Sheet 1 (New York: United Nations).

UN (2002n) *National Institutions for the Promotion and Protection of Human Rights* (New York: United Nations).

UN (2002o) *Protection of the Heritage of Indigenous Peoples*, Human Rights Study Series, No. 10 (New York: United Nations).

UN (2002p) *The Rights of Indigenous Peoples*, Fact Sheet 9 (New York: United Nations).

UN (2002q) *The Rights of Migrant Workers*, Fact Sheet 24 (New York: United Nations).

UN (2002r) *Selected Decisions of the Human Rights Committee under the Optional Protocol* (New York: United Nations).

UN (2002s) *Seventeen Frequently Asked Questions about United Nations Special Rapporteurs*, Fact Sheet 27 (New York: United Nations).

UN (2002t) *Study on the Rights of Persons belonging to Ethnic, Religious and Linguistic Minorities*, Human Rights Study Series, No. 5 (New York: United Nations).

UN (2002u) *United Nations Action in the Field of Human Rights* (New York: United Nations).

UNHCR (2000) *Repatriation and Rehabilitation* (New York: UNHCR).

UNHCR (2001) *The State of the World's Refugees* (New York: UNHCR).

UNHCR (2002) *Global Report 2001* (New York: UNHCR).

UNICEF (1999) *Human Rights for Children and Women: How UNICEF Makes Them a Reality* (New York: UNICEF).

UNRWA (UN Relief and Works Agency) (2000) *Palestinian Refugees* (New York: UNRWA).

US Department of State (2001) *Annual Report on International Religious Freedom* (Washington: US Govt).

Villa-Vincencio, Charles (1999) *A Theology of Reconstruction: Nation-Building and Human Rights* (Cambridge: Cambridge University Press).

Wade, Davis (2001) *Light at the Edge of the World: A Journey through the Realm of Vanishing Cultures* (London: Bloomsbury).

Waller, James (2002) *Becoming Evil: How Ordinary People Commit Genocide and Mass Killing* (Oxford: Oxford University Press).

Walvin, James (2001) *Black Ivory: A History of British Slavery* (Malden, MA: Blackwell Publishers).

Webb, W.L. and Rose Bell (1997) *An Embarrassment of Tyrannies: Twenty-Five Years of Index on Censorship* (London: Victor Gollancz).

Weine, Stevan M. (1999) *When History is a Nightmare: Lives and Memories of Ethnic Cleansing in Bosnia-Herzogovina* (New Brunswick, NJ: Rutgers University Press).

Wellman, Carl (2000) *The Proliferation of Rights: Moral Progress or Empty Rhetoric?* (Oxford: Westview).

Went, Robert (2000) *Globalization: Neoliberal Challenge, Radical Response* (Sterling, VA: Pluto).

Wichterich, Christa (2000) *The Globalised Woman: Reports from the Future of Inequality*, trans. Patrick Camiller (London: Zed Books).

Wright, A. (2000) 'The Spiritual Education Project', in M. Grimmit (ed.) *Pedagogies of Religious Education: Case Studies in the Research and Development of Good Pedagogic Practice* (Great Wakering: McCrimmons).

Index

aboriginal peoples *see* indigenous peoples
Advisory Group on Citizenship: QCA 11
Africa: human rights organisations 38, 40, 42;
    refugees 96, 97
Americas: human rights organisations 40, 42;
    refugees 96; religious freedom 130–1
Anti-Slavery International 106
apartheid *see* indigenous peoples; racial
    discrimination
approaches: RE teaching 14
armed conflict *see* war and armed conflict
arts: freedom of expression 116–18
Asia: human rights organisations 40, 42;
    refugees 97
assessment: planning 73–5
asylum 91–103; attainment targets 98;
    attitudes 99–100; historical-legal-political
    background 91–7; international legal
    standards 92–5; National Curriculum
    citizenship links 100–1; planning notes
    98–102; United Nations 92–7; world hot
    spots 96–7
atrocities 1, 2, 29, *see also* genocide
attainment targets: asylum 98; economic
    rights and environmental responsibilities
    147; freedom of expression 121; freedom
    of religion and belief 134; genocide 85–6;
    rights of indigenous peoples 171; slavery
    109–10; women's rights 159
attitudes: asylum 99–100; economic rights
    and environmental responsibilities
    148–9; freedom of expression 122;
    freedom of religion and belief 135;
    genocide 87; rights of indigenous peoples
    173; slavery 110–11; women's rights
    160–1
audit: school provision for participation 64

Beijing World Conference on Women (1995)
    153, 156–7
benefits of citizenship education: Crick
    Report 11–12
Beth Shalom Holocaust Centre 84
bonded labour 106

Capacity 2015: UNDP 144
caste system 105
celebration of achievements 72
censorship 115–18, 120, 125, *see also* freedom
    of expression
Centre for Citizenship Studies in Education
    68
children: celebration of achievements 72;
    child labour 54, 107; girls' rights 157;
    maternity and upbringing 155;
    participation skills 12, 61–9; rights 51–4;
    sexual exploitation 106, 107; slavery 106,
    107
Christianity 29, 116–17, 174
citizenship teaching: GCSE 74; guidance
    sources 55
City of God (Saint Augustine) 2
colonialism 48, 128, 140, 165, 174, *see also*
    imperialism; postcolonial influences
Commonwealth 38, 39
community involvement: Crick Report
    12; participation 64; success factors
    69–72
Community Partners initiative 65, 69
conflict: economic rights and environmental
    responsibilities 139, 147; QCA citizenship
    unit 14, 15–21; religious/cultural/ethnic
    83; world events 1, 2, *see also* genocide; war
    and armed conflict
Convention on the Elimination of All Forms